HEARST MARINE BOOKS
COMPLETE GUIDE TO BOAT MAINTENANCE AND REPAIR

HEARST MARINE BOOKS COMPLETE GUIDE TO BOAT MAINTENANCE AND REPAIR

David G. Brown

Illustrations by Ron Carboni

HEARST MARINE BOOKS
New York

It is the policy of William Morrow and Company, Inc., and its imprints and affiliates, recognizing the importance of preserving what has been written, to print the books we publish on acid-free paper, and we exert our best efforts to that end.

Library of Congress Cataloging-in-Publication Data

Brown, David G. (David Geren), 1944—
    Hearst Marine Books complete guide to boat maintenance & repair / by David G. Brown.
        p.   cm.
    Includes index.
    ISBN 0-688-11932-8
    1. Boats and boating—Maintenance and repair. I. Title.
II. Title: Complete guide to boat maintenance & repair.
VM322.B76   1993
623.8′2′0288—dc20   93-3394
                                                   CIP

Printed in the United States of America

First Edition

1 2 3 4 5 6 7 8 9 10

BOOK DESIGN BY GIORGETTA BELL MCREE

This book is dedicated to my late father, the *real* Charlie Brown, who actually did sink a box kite in Peck's Pond off the back of a 13-foot Lyman. During our thirty-some seasons together he passed his love of the water and of working on boats to me. He got me started by allowing me to make mistakes.

FOREWORD

Six inches of snow lie on the lawn and more is scudding across ice-crusted Sandusky Bay. Today is truly the dark of winter, not the kind of day when most people think of boats. Yet this blustery afternoon is as much a part of my boating season as any sunny July afternoon. Summer is blooming in my workshop, where a third coat of varnish is drying on the coaming boards of my 19-foot Typhoon sailboat. The pleasant exertion of sanding those boards has warmed many afternoons this winter. Now the amber glow of fresh varnish hints of summer days to come.

Winter has been part of my boating season since a day in 1948 when my father dragged home an aging wooden boat. That boat needed a winter of work just to float. In the years since, my family has owned a dozen boats: five powerboats, four sailboats, and three dinghies of various purpose. Working on those boats has been a major part of

the joy of ownership. I spent hours as a youngster alongside my father as we scraped, sanded, and varnished. Those are golden memories now that both my dad and those boats are gone. In fact, my memories of those hours are brighter than my recollections of family vacation cruises.

Prior to mass marketing of boats in the 1980s, boat ownership involved a lot more than just opening a checkbook. In the 1950s and sixties, owners still took an active part in the upkeep and maintenance of their vessels. Their willingness to paint or caulk had nothing to do with money. It was pride. I've scraped bottom paint alongside company presidents, doctors, and lawyers. Those men taught me that what you get out of owning a boat (or anything else) is directly related to the effort you put into it. That's what this book is all about: *getting more out of your boat by putting more of yourself into it.*

HOW TO USE THIS BOOK

This is not a text on how to become a professional boat repairman or a boat builder. Rather, it is designed for the weekend warrior, who looks to his boat for pleasant diversion from the frustrations of the workaday world. The projects presented here can be accomplished by a reasonably coordinated worker with tools from Sears. Many projects can be finished in less than an hour. All jobs can be brought to a stopping point in four hours or less, if the work must be spread out over several weekends.

Required tools, materials, and time estimates given at the start of each project are intended to help prepare for the task at hand and to plan how much time to allot. It's not a good idea to purchase materials in advance by just consulting the list. It's often better to hold off purchasing some materials until far enough along with the job to know exactly what is needed.

Time estimates given in this book are just that: estimates. Each boat is unique. Replacing a cleat on one boat may take half an hour, while two hours aren't long enough on another craft. Work always takes longer than planned, so have more time available than the minimum estimate. Above all, don't rush. Let the work choose its own speed.

Professional boat craftsmen "measure twice and cut once." This is sage advice. Check and double-check measurements before drilling or cutting. Getting a second opinion isn't a bad idea when it comes to drilling holes in the hull below the waterline. Paper or cardboard templates should be made when fitting new furniture into the hull. A mistake on cardboard costs only a few cents, but it can mean a cost of a hundred dollars or more if you ruin a sheet of teak veneer marine plywood.

Finally, enjoy what you are doing . . . both when things go right *and* when you make mistakes. Everything (even a big hole in the bottom) can be repaired. Occasionally stand back to admire your work as the job progresses. As each step is completed the project takes on a life of its own. The feeling of accomplishment should be more than enough compensation for the energy expended.

ACKNOWLEDGMENTS

This book would not exist without the assistance and constant encouragement of my wife, Carol. I would also like to thank my mother, Emma Brown, and Joanne Sutton for their assistance proofreading and correcting rough drafts of the manuscript. And without the help of master boat carpenter Richard Minier, many parts of this book could not have been written.

CONTENTS

HEARST MARINE BOOKS COMPLETE GUIDE TO BOAT MAINTENANCE AND REPAIR

INTRODUCTION

THE TOOLBOX

Every boat should carry a basic tool kit containing a minimum set of tools for emergency repairs on the boat's engine, electrical system, and plumbing. A more extensive selection of tools is needed to make serious repairs or improvements. Exactly which to choose is a matter of personal preference. Even professionals disagree over tools. One worker may prefer a folding carpenter's ruler while another swears by a steel tape measure. Both get the job done equally well.

Toolboxes

Metal toolboxes have sharp corners that gouge, nick, and scrape decks, bulkheads, and topsides. Professional boat repairmen avoid metal boxes because of the damage they can do. One way to tame a metal box is to glue a scrap of carpet to the bottom to protect woodwork and gel coat. The best boxes for marine use are made of industrial-grade plastic, which doesn't dent or scratch. At least one manufacturer produces a box with a "waterproof" seal specifically for boats. Marine catalogues list canvas tool bags for sale. Bags are very nautical but not practical, since they roll over and dump tools everywhere.

HAND TOOLS

Screwdrivers

Good screwdrivers have comfortable handles made of impact-resistant plastic or wood. The metal shank should be well set into the handle in

Suggested Basic Toolbox Contents

Screwdrivers: Three straight-slot of various sizes plus a no. 1, no. 2, and no. 3 Phillips.

Pliers: Regular 8-inch slip-joint; diagonal cutters and possibly arc joint ("water pump") pliers.

Wrenches: Set of basic combination box/end wrenches in standard and metric sizes. Optional: a ⅜-inch-drive socket set with ratchet.

Chisels: Two brand-name chisels with plastic handles. Start with ¼- and ½-inch widths.

Saws: One toolbox-size compass-saw nest and one hacksaw with spare blades.

Other Hand Tools: Claw hammer, knife, measuring tape or folding rule, combination square, bevel gauge, scratch awl, and compass.

Drill Motor: 115-volt corded drill with: set of twist drills from 1/32 to ¼ inch; speed bores from ¼ to 1 inch; no. 6, no. 8, and no. 10 wood screw pilot bits.

Saber Saw: 115-volt corded model with a selection of wood- and metal-cutting blades.

such a way that it will not "spin out" under high torque. Square or hexagonal shanks allow the use of an end wrench to increase turning force when necessary.

Straight-Slot Screwdrivers: These are the most common variety. Tips should be absolutely square to the shanks and straight across. They should fit screw slots exactly. Sloppiness or "play" will strip the edges of the slots. Blade widths of ⅛, 3/16, ¼, and 5/16 inch are common.

Phillips Screwdrivers: The tip is cross-shaped. Most stainless-steel screws used on boats have Phillips heads. Screw slots and screwdriver tips are matched by size starting with number 0 (zero) at the small end and going up to the two-fisted number 4. Buy Phillips sizes numbers 2 and 3 for most jobs and possibly number 1 or, rarely, a number 0 for electronics work.

Torx Screwdrivers: Robot assembly of automobiles brought about the star-shaped Torx screw slot and driver tip. So far, these have seen only the most limited use on boats. Sizes range from T-10 at the small end to T-30 at the large.

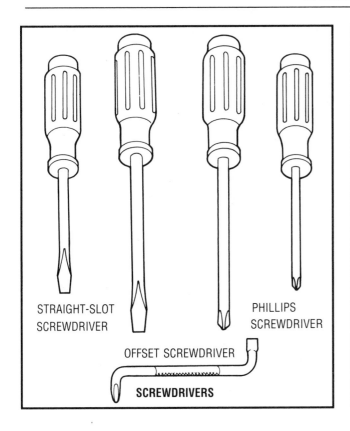

STRAIGHT-SLOT
SCREWDRIVER

PHILLIPS
SCREWDRIVER

OFFSET SCREWDRIVER

SCREWDRIVERS

Pliers

Pliers are mechanical devices that amplify the natural grip of the human hand. For such simple tools, they come in a bewildering variety of types and sizes.

Slip-Joint Pliers: These are the standard pliers everyone has used. The slip joint gives the jaws two different grip ranges. Six- and 8-inch sizes are the most useful.

Arc-Joint Pliers: Often called "water pump pliers," these have long handles and an arc joint that allows a wide variation in grip size. Useful for larger jobs than can be handled by regular pliers.

Needle-Nose Pliers: These have long, pointed jaws, and are an absolute necessity for electrical work. Useless for holding nuts or other jobs normally done with regular pliers. Some versions incorporate a wire cutter.

PLIERS

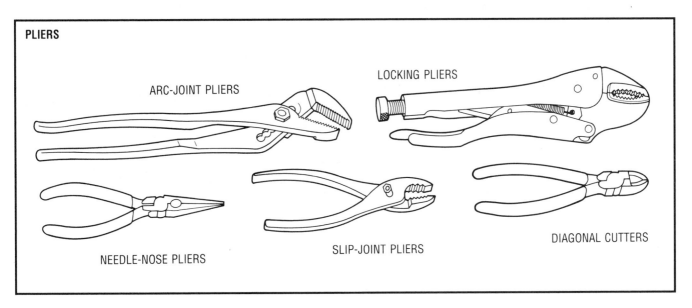

ARC-JOINT PLIERS

LOCKING PLIERS

NEEDLE-NOSE PLIERS

SLIP-JOINT PLIERS

DIAGONAL CUTTERS

Locking Pliers: The original (and still best) are the famous Vice Grips brand. An adjusting screw "locks" them in position on a nut or pipe. Enough force can be generated to destroy the sharp edges of nuts, but this may be acceptable in some situations.

Diagonal Cutters: Universally known as "dikes" by electronics technicians and as "wire cutters" by everyone else, these pliers are designed only for cutting or skinning wire.

Wrenches

Wrenches are a general class of tools designed to tighten or loosen fasteners or threaded fittings by turning. They come in both standard (fractional inch or "English") and in metric sizes. Cheap wrenches abound, which may explain why so many weekend mechanics have skinned knuckles.

End Wrenches: Flat bars of steel with U-shaped openings designed to fit nuts of specific size. Called "spanners" in England, end wrenches have the widest variety of applications.

Box Wrenches: Sisters to end wrenches, these have loops of metal at each end cut to fit specific size nuts. Box wrenches are less likely to slip or round off nuts.

Combination Wrenches: Box and end wrenches combined into one tool. Both ends of the tool fit the same size nut. Combination wrenches are a "best buy" for the weekend warrior.

Adjustable Wrenches: These are end wrenches with a movable jaw that allows a variety of nut sizes to be accommodated by one wrench. Adjustable wrenches tend to round off the corners of nuts in high-torque situations. Always tighten *toward* the adjustable jaw. Buy a 6-inch and an 8-inch size.

Socket Wrenches: The stock-in-trade of serious mechanics, sockets are accurately broached to fit over specific size nuts. A square drive hole in the top of the socket allows turning with either a ratchet handle or what is popularly known as a "breaker bar." Extensions and universal joints allow turning nuts in tight locations. Special deep sockets allow the turning of a nut on a protruding bolt.

Allen Wrenches: Also known as "hex keys," these fit into hexagonal recesses in the heads of set screws and other fittings. Sets of loose keys in a pouch always seem to lack the one needed. Buy a set in which the wrenches are captive in a metal handle.

Pipe Wrench: Seldom used on boats, but may be useful in some engine applications.

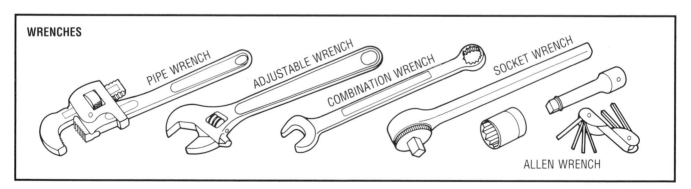

WRENCHES

PIPE WRENCH • ADJUSTABLE WRENCH • COMBINATION WRENCH • SOCKET WRENCH • ALLEN WRENCH

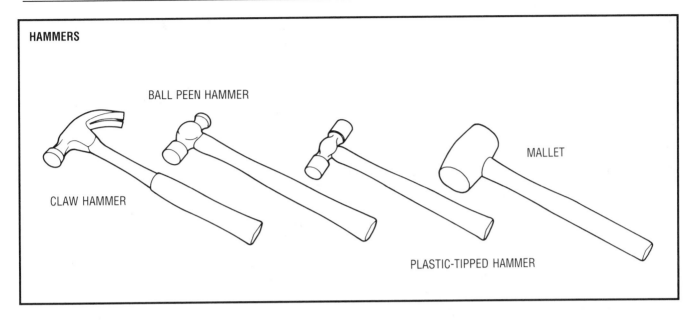

HAMMERS

BALL PEEN HAMMER

CLAW HAMMER

MALLET

PLASTIC-TIPPED HAMMER

Hammers

There's an old joke that everything fits when hit by a big enough hammer. In truth, craftsmen avoid forcing anything on boats. Still, hammers have a place in every nautical toolbox.

Claw Hammer: The 16-ounce carpenter's hammer is most useful. Look for a curved claw hammer with a notch in the claw for removing small nails. Rip or framing hammers are too heavy for boat work.

Ball Peen Hammer: Also known as a "machinist's hammer," it has a round knob on the back side instead of a nail claw. The knob (technically, the "peen") is used to form metal while the striking face is used like a regular hammer. A 12-ounce hammer is big enough.

Mallet: This tool has a large rubber head designed not to dent or scratch when used to drive wooden parts together. A rubber mallet filled with lead shot is known as a "dead blow hammer" since it does not bounce back when struck.

Plastic-Tipped Hammer: The most important use for this type of hammer is sounding hulls during surveys. It can deliver a forceful blow without denting or scratching the surface. It may also be used to drive a wood chisel without damaging that tool's handle.

Wooden Maul: Used by wood-carvers to drive chisels; necessary only for carving a figurehead.

Caulking Hammer: Also known as a caulking (pronounced "corking") maul, this very specialized hammer is traditionally used to caulk the underwater seams of wooden boats. A good decoration for rec room walls.

Handsaws

Despite the proliferation of electric saws, old-fashioned handsaws are still an important part of every toolbox. Two handsaws are needed, one to cut wood and another to cut metal.

WOOD-CUTTING SAWS

Crosscut Saw: Has large, widely spaced teeth designed to cut *across* the grain of the wood.

Ripsaw: Has smaller, closer-spaced teeth designed to cut *with* the grain of the wood.

Toolbox Saw: A half-size saw with combination teeth designed to allow crosscutting or ripping. The length of the blade allows this saw to fit inside larger toolboxes, hence the name.

Keyhole (or Compass) Saw: Usually sold as a "nest" of saws, with several blades that fit a single handle. Pointed blades allow you to start a cut from a drilled hole. A good nest of saws is handy to have aboard a boat in place of larger, traditional saws.

Backsaw: A short saw with a metal rib along the non-cutting top edge to stiffen the blade. Used almost exclusively to cut miters in a miter box.

METAL-CUTTING SAWS

Hacksaw: The traditional metal-cutting saw. It consists of a substantial metal frame that supports a disposable blade. Special blades are available for various metals.

Blade Handle: Used in confined areas to cut using only one end of a hacksaw blade without the large metal supporting frame. The handle allows the blade to be held comfortably, but does not support the cutting portion of the blade. Broken and bent blades are a common result.

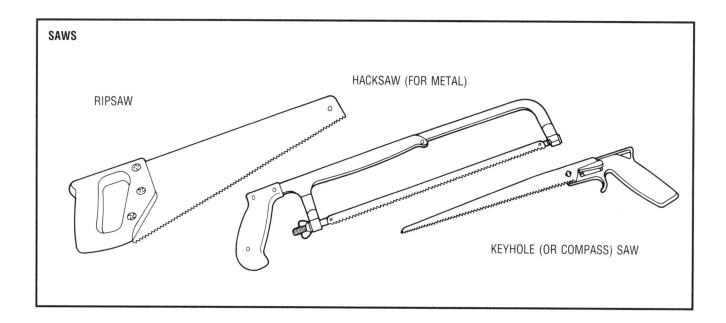

SAWS

RIPSAW

HACKSAW (FOR METAL)

KEYHOLE (OR COMPASS) SAW

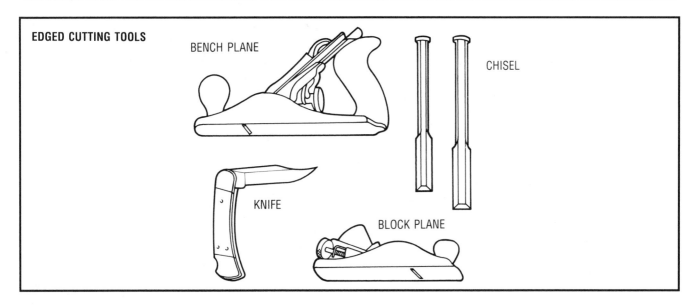

EDGED CUTTING TOOLS

BENCH PLANE

CHISEL

KNIFE

BLOCK PLANE

Edged Cutting Tools

Edged tools separate would-be craftsmen from true wood butchers. Wood chisels and planes take skill to use properly. The only way to gain this skill is to grab a tool and begin making chips. The frustrating process of learning to guide a sharp edge through wood is worth the effort. No tools give as much satisfaction for a job well done as planes and chisels.

Chisels: Don't spend money on anything less than the best available wood chisels. Look for forged steel blades well set into wood or plastic handles. Common sizes are ¼, ½, ¾, and 1 inch.

Wood Planes: A plane is just a wide chisel set in a metal frame that insures the blade always strikes the wood at the same angle. Serious woodworkers use a variety of planes, but only the 6-inch block plane is necessary.

Block Plane: A small plane with a body approximately 6½ inches long and a blade about 1½ inches wide. Useful for trimming the ends (across the grain) of cut pieces or for planing with the grain when fitting smaller items. Stores easily.

Bench Plane: A medium-size plane, usually 9 to 10 inches long, with a 2-inch-wide blade. Used to smooth edges or flat surfaces with the grain.

Knives: The traditional toolbox knife has replaceable blades. A good 4-inch-blade pocketknife is also handy.

Sharpening Stones: Edged tools are only as good as they are sharp. A variety of sharpening stones and tool-holding systems are available today. Pick a stone and system and learn how to use it.

Measuring Tools

There is hardly a job that doesn't require you to measure either a length or an angle (or both). The most common measuring device is the ubiquitous steel tape. Professional boat workers seem to favor old-fashioned folding wooden rules. This is another area where personal choice is the deciding factor. An inch is an inch. As for angles, every boat toolbox needs at least one square and a bevel gauge.

Steel Tape: Most measuring tapes are spring-loaded, so they automatically retract into their cases. Tapes over ¾ inch wide are preferred because they are stiff enough when unrolled to measure distances somewhat beyond an arm's length.

Wooden Folding Rule: The classic carpenter's rule is popular with professionals because it is self-supporting when extended. Avoid cheap rules, as their joints soon wear and measurements become erratic. A good rule has a brass extension allowing accurate inside measurements.

Metal Straight Ruler: Comes in lengths from 1 to 8 feet. Short ones are handy when laying out jobs on the workbench. Longer rulers can double as a straightedge when marking cut lines on plywood panels.

Try Square: Squares are used less often on boats than in home construction. Few parts of a boat are square except for doors, drawers, and other pieces of furniture. An 8-inch try square fits nicely into most boxes and is a handy tool. It can be replaced by a combination square.

Combination Square: This square consists of a metal rule (usually a foot long) that slides in a handle that always remains square to the rule. It is useful for measuring depths or marking cut lines at a constant distance from the edge of a board.

Bevel Gauge: This is essentially a try square that can be adjusted to any angle. It is useful for taking angles off the boat and transferring them to the work for accurate reproduction.

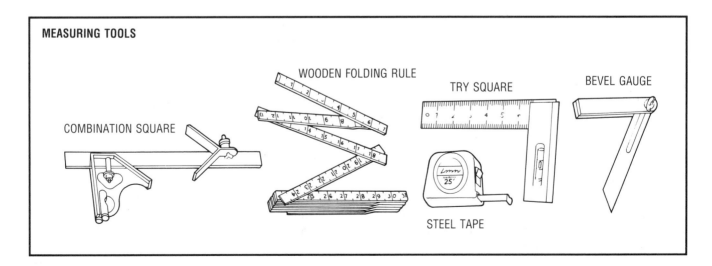

MEASURING TOOLS

WOODEN FOLDING RULE

TRY SQUARE

BEVEL GAUGE

COMBINATION SQUARE

STEEL TAPE

Miscellaneous Hand Tools

C-Clamps: There are never too many clamps for a glue job. C-clamps come in a variety of sizes, but the most useful are in the 3-to-6-inch range.

Center Punch: Used to mark a dimple in metal to guide the drill when making holes.

Cotter Pin Puller: Looking like a bent screwdriver, this tool makes pulling reluctant cotter pins easy. Sailors especially appreciate this tool when working on rigging.

Hand-Crank Drill: Maybe it looks old-fashioned, but an "egg beater" drill never electrocuted anyone around the water. It works without extension cords and its battery never runs down. Holes of up to ¼ inch in diameter can be drilled by hand through wood, fiberglass, and aluminum.

Folding Ladder: Working on boats stored ashore always involves climbing. Modern folding aluminum ladders can be used for climbing aboard or can be set up as scaffolding.

Level: A 24-inch carpenter's level is handy when setting furniture in a properly leveled boat. It can also be used as a straightedge.

Miter Box: This is a guide for cutting accurate 45-degree angles for miters. Simple miter boxes are just slotted wooden devices. More complex tools actually guide the saw in metal slides.

Rivet Gun: This tool is used to set so-called blind or Pop rivets of aluminum, steel, or stainless steel. Cheap rivet tools wear out quickly, especially when setting stainless-steel rivets, which are common on sailboat rigging.

Scratch Awl: This pointed "ice pick" tool is used to mark cut lines on wood for maximum accuracy. It is also handy in surveying wooden boats.

Tap and Die Sets: Taps cut threads on the inside of holes in metal while dies cut threads on the outside of metal rods. Sizes 4-40, 6-32, 8-32, 10-32, 10-24, and ¼-20 match standard stainless-steel machine screws used on boats.

Tin Snips: Heavy-duty scissors designed to cut thin metal. Aircraft snips are expensive, but they make cutting easier.

Tubing Cutter: The sharp wheel of this tool makes a smooth, straight cut on copper, brass, and aluminum tubing. This tool is necessary for serious plumbing jobs.

Voltmeter (Multimeter): This instrument measures the voltage on an electrical circuit. Many also have an ohm scale, which can be used to trace open circuits.

ELECTRIC HAND TOOLS

Electric hand tools save labor, but the drill or sander that speeds up the work also speeds up the mistakes. That's why professional boat workers still use hand tools ten-to-one over power tools for critical work. Until a few years ago, the term *power tool* implied a long extension cord plugged into a 115-volt outlet. "Corded" tools still are the backbone of the power tool world, but battery tools are growing in both capability and popularity. A mid-priced battery drill is excellent for working around the water because it doesn't use potentially deadly house current. Most battery drill motors can adequately power bits of up to ¼ inch in metal or fiberglass and ⅜ inch in wood.

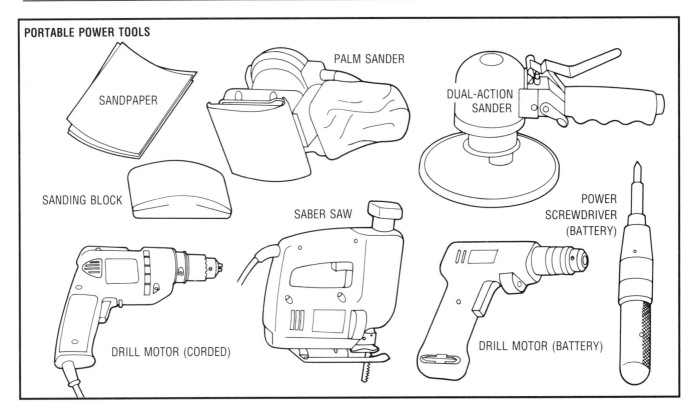

PORTABLE POWER TOOLS

SANDPAPER

PALM SANDER

DUAL-ACTION SANDER

SANDING BLOCK

POWER SCREWDRIVER (BATTERY)

SABER SAW

DRILL MOTOR (CORDED)

DRILL MOTOR (BATTERY)

Portable Power Tools

Drill Motor (corded): This is the basic electric hand tool. Buy a "professional" model with at least a ⅜-inch chuck. Look for a minimum 4-amp motor turning a top speed of 2,500 rpm. Variable speed and the ability to operate in reverse are almost mandatory features.

Drill Motor (battery): Professional battery tools are too expensive for the home worker. A better value is a mid-cost tool with at least a 6.3-volt motor. A ⅜-inch chuck is desirable. Reversing and variable speed are mandatory for using this tool as a power screwdriver.

Power Screwdriver: A corded version is unnecessary except for professional boat building. Battery-powered versions eliminate the drudgery of driving screws. Buy the unit with the biggest battery (in both volts and amps) affordable. Big batteries last longer between recharges.

Saber Saw (corded): Avoid the home workshop versions of this tool as they fail quickly in hard service. Buy at least a low-end professional model with variable speed, variable blade orbit, and scrolling. At least a ⅓-horsepower motor is necessary for cutting heavy plywood and thick fiberglass laminates.

Portable Circular Saw (corded): Although more powerful and able to cut thicker stock, this tool is less helpful around boats than a good saber saw. The standard construction saw uses a 7¼-inch blade. A 2-horsepower motor is not too small.

Palm ("Jitterbug") Sander (corded): This type of electric sander uses a quarter sheet of standard sandpaper. It moves the pad in a rapid orbit, producing a smooth finish. Once again, avoid tools intended for the home workshop. Professional palm sanders cut faster and last longer and are only slightly more expensive. The best have a dust collection system.

Pad Sander (corded): Using either one half or one third of a standard sheet of sandpaper, the pad sander offers either orbital or straight-line motion for sanding. Straight-line motion is used for finish sanding to eliminate cross-grain scratches. Beware of low-cost sanders that *look* like straight-line pad sanders but in fact provide orbital action only.

Belt Sander (corded): In the wrong hands, a portable belt sander is a real boat killer. It can cut deep gouges before the uninitiated operator even knows he's in trouble. No other tool levels and smoothes a planked wood deck faster.

Disc Sander/Polisher (corded): Professionals use these with wool bonnets to polish boat hulls. Since low speeds are needed to avoid damaging fiberglass gel coat, look for variable speed or a top speed of 2,000 rpm. Buy as much horsepower as can be comfortably lifted.

Dual-Action Sander: Known as a "D-A," this circular sander simultaneously rotates and orbits the sanding pad to produce a swirl-free finish. Air-powered D-A's are common in professional shops. Newer, electric D-A sanders offer the same advantages without the need for an air compressor. Buy the largest diameter sanding pad available.

Router (corded): Some craftsmen use a router in place of a saw when cutting thin material such as plywood. A router is necessary for advanced work such as dovetail joints. This tool requires considerable skill to use correctly and is not necessary for most boat maintenance and repairs. Buy a router only if it is needed.

Wet/Dry Vacuum (corded): Cleanup is the hardest part of any job. A good wet/dry vacuum does away with most of the drudgery. A vacuum also comes in handy for drying out bilge sumps—just suck up the water! For boat work, a smaller vacuum is more useful than a big one on account of the limited working space and the problem of carrying it up ladders.

BENCH POWER TOOLS

Bench tools range from the common table saw to exotic reciprocating drum sanders. A fully equipped boat shop will have tens of thousands of dollars in large power tools. While many of these might be useful to the weekend boatwright, their cost does not justify purchase. A good home workshop needs only a table saw and a drill press. The serious amateur may want to add a small band saw and perhaps a disc-belt sander.

Table Saw: This tool consists of a circular saw blade set into a table. The blade should tilt (with a tilting arbor) for bevel cuts and the table should be slotted for a miter gauge. The saw should have a rip fence. At least a 1-horsepower motor is needed on an 8-inch saw and a 2-horsepower motor on a 10-inch machine.

Radial-Arm Saw: This is really a portable circular saw fixed to a sliding carriage on an overhead beam. Excellent control over the position and travel of the blade is possible. The width of stock that can be cut is limited by the travel of the saw on the beam. Optional accessories are similar to those for a table saw.

Band Saw: Boatyards that build wooden vessels have huge band saws to resaw wood flitches into planks. In the home shop, band saws are most often used to cut curves and small patterns out of flat stock.

Jointer-Planer: This tool puts a flat, straight edge on a plank and can be used to smooth plane planks up to the width of the cutter blades. Needed only for serious woodworking projects.

Disc-Belt Sander: This bench machine has an adjustable table and various guides to hold the work. Accurate edges, angles, and surfaces can be sanded with care. A 6-inch disc coupled with a 4-inch belt is the minimum size machine to purchase.

Drill Press: Necessary for accurate drilling of holes in metal or wood, a drill press can also be used for sanding and planing with the appropriate accessories. A 10-inch drill powered by a ¼-horsepower motor is big enough for the home shop. A bench model is just as good as a floor-stand drill press but costs a bit less.

SAFETY ON THE JOB

Professional boat builders and craftsmen are becoming increasingly safety conscious. Rubber gloves, safety goggles, respirators, and hearing protectors now appear in tool kits alongside hammers and screwdrivers. There are good reasons why safety equipment is becoming standard equipment for boat workers. Many of the raw materials, paints, and chemicals that are used to build or repair modern boats present safety hazards to unprotected workers.

Acetone, MEK, isocyanates, and similar chemicals can damage the skin or eyes and may be toxic to breathe. Some chemicals are also suspected of causing cancer with long-term exposure. That said, don't be afraid to work on boats. Safety equipment is neither difficult to obtain nor expensive.

And although appropriate eye and skin protection will never go out of style, it appears that working on boats will be much safer in the near future. Commercial substitutes for flammable and dangerous solvents such as acetone and paint thinner are already on the market. Unfortunately, these products are currently packaged in industrial-sized containers only, but look for them to appear on chandlery shelves in a few years.

WEST System already markets a biodegradable cleaning solution for removing uncured resin from tools. Z-Spar has just introduced a water-based marine varnish that has no volatile organic solvents. Look for more water-based finishes to appear before the end of the decade as environmental laws get tougher on old-fashioned solvent-based paints and coatings.

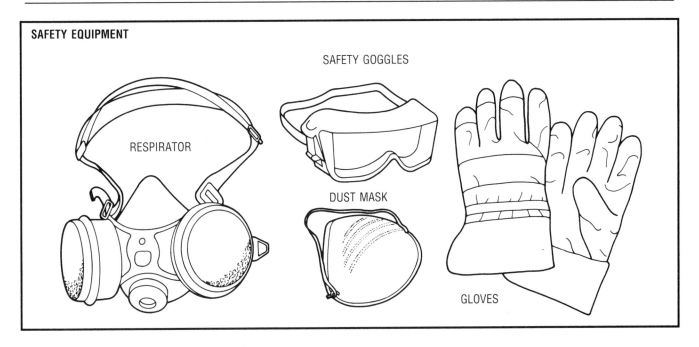

SAFETY EQUIPMENT

SAFETY GOGGLES

RESPIRATOR

DUST MASK

GLOVES

Eye Safety

Eye protection is provided by face shields, goggles, or spectacles. The type of protection chosen depends upon the job and the nature of the potential injuries. One word of caution to anyone who wears prescription glasses: reading glasses may be called "unbreakable" but they do not meet specifications for true safety glasses. Street glasses cannot be counted on to provide sufficient protection against impact.

Face Shields: These protect both eyes and face from harm. Good shields curve completely around the face, protecting it from the front and sides. Look for one that is at least 6 inches long and 0.04 inches thick.

Safety Goggles: There are special safety goggles for just about every job. Amateur boatwrights normally need a pair made of clear, flexible plastic. (The exception is welding, which requires special protection.) Goggles sized for men may be grossly oversized for a petite woman, who should check size before buying. Goggles should meet the requirements of the ANSI Z87-1-1979 standard.

Safety Spectacles: For some reason, safety specialists use the quaint name of "spectacles" for what everyone else calls "safety glasses." Tempered safety glass or high-impact plastic lenses give the same protection, but glass lenses are far less vulnerable to scratches. Spectacles should meet the ANSI Z87-1-1979 standard.

Table 1.1

SUGGESTED EYE PROTECTION

Task	Danger	Protective Device
Mixing or Using Chemicals	Splashes	Face Shield
Applying Resin to Glass Cloth	Splashes	Face Shield or Goggles with Side Shields
Drilling or Cutting Fiberglass	Particles and Dust	Goggles or Spectacles with Side Shields
Scraping Paint off Bottom	Particles	Goggles or Spectacles with Side Shields
Power Wire Brush or Flap Wheel	Particles and Dust	Face Shield
Power Wood Tools	Particles and Dust	Goggles or Spectacles with Side Shields
Grinding Metal	Particles Dust and Sparks	Face Shield
Drilling Metal	Flying Chips	Goggles or Spectacles with Side Shields
Cleaning Teak	Splashes	Goggles or Spectacles with Side Shields
Painting (Brush)	Splashes	Goggles or Spectacles with Side Shields
Painting (Spray)	Airborne Paint	Special Goggles or Face Shield
Welding	Sparks and UV Light	Special Welding Goggles

Breathing Protection

Chemicals and solvents used in modern boat repairs often give off fumes or gasses that range from mildly irritating to downright toxic. Dust created by sanding antifouling paint contains strong copper or tin biocide (see page 68). Even seemingly innocuous wood-sanding dust has been implicated in certain types of lung cancer. Faced with this sort of work environment, it's no wonder that professional boat craftsmen are always reaching for a dust mask or respirator.

Dust Masks and Respirators: Dust masks filter irritating dust out of the air. They are effective in preventing sanding dust and sawdust from entering the lungs but are useless against airborne chemicals and toxic fumes.

Dust respirators are similar, except that they are capable of filtering out more harmful dust and particles. A good dust respirator may also protect against some types of airborne mists such as paint overspray.

Chemical Respirators: Combine a dust filter with a special cartridge designed to remove harmful chemical vapors from the air. The most expensive have rubber masks with replaceable filters and cartridges. Not found at neighborhood hardware stores, they are available from auto parts stores that sell auto refinishing supplies. Get cartridges intended for paint, lacquer and enamel mists, organic vapors, pesticides, dust, and fumes.

Skin Protection

Solvents, resins, and sealants used on fiberglass boats are skin irritants. Anyone who has worked with fiberglass has experienced "glass itch," which is caused by almost microscopic pieces of fiberglass that get imbedded in the skin. This itch is often accompanied by a mild rash. Time is the only cure; eventually the glass fibers wear out of the skin and the itching stops. There's no reason to go through this mild agony. Both the itch and the rash can be prevented by proper skin protection.

HAND PROTECTION

Household rubber gloves give some protection, but they wear out quickly when exposed to industrial solvents. Instead, visit a local auto parts store for a pair of Du Pont M-116 Hand Protection Chemical Solution Gloves, which will outlast a dozen pair of ordinary rubber gloves.

For small jobs, cheap disposable rubber or plastic gloves are the answer. The least expensive are medical "examination gloves" sold by most drug stores. Exam gloves don't fit anyone's hand very well, but they're good enough for holding a paint brush, rubbing out stain, or cleaning a small piece of teak.

Canvas or leather work gloves provide good protection when handling heavy, rough items like cement blocks. Leather gloves are a good way to prevent splinters from plywood or rough sawn lumber.

HEAD AND HAIR PROTECTION

Anyone who has sanded the bottom of a boat knows the definition of *dirty*. Even when you're wearing a mask and goggles, dust gets into your hair and onto your skin. Hair catches the most dust simply because the sanding is almost always done overhead. A cheap way to keep dust and paint chips out of the hair is to purchase a spray painter's "spray sock." This is a knitted helmet that fits tightly to head and neck. It leaves an opening for the face, so goggles and a mask are still necessary. Spray socks are available from automotive paint stores.

Another good protective device is a traditional sailor's watch cap. It can be pulled down over the back of your neck and ears to duplicate most of the protection of a "spray sock." The best part of a watch cap, however, is its warmth. Nothing keeps feet warmer on an early spring day than a watch cap.

BODY PROTECTION

Weekend chore clothing is generally adequate when working on a boat. Avoid loose-fitting garments as well as scarves and other items that could become caught in machinery. Jewelry also can be dangerous around machines, so forgo baubles and bangles.

Rubber-soled deck shoes offer good footing but little other protection. "Boatyard boots" are leather high-top construction boots that have white rubber soles. They shrug off water, give good footing, and don't leave black marks on decks and topsides. These boots are generally sized to accommodate two pair of socks for warmth in cool spring or fall weather.

Long sleeves and buttoned collars fend off fiberglass dust with its accompanying skin irritation and rash. Clothing soiled with fiberglass dust should first be shaken outdoors and then washed separately. Start with a soak cycle and finish with a regular wash. Do not wash other garments together with fiberglass-soiled work clothes. It is possible to spread the fiberglass dust into the uncontaminated clothing. Also, running the washer through a "dummy" wash cycle with no clothes in it is a good way to be sure that all fiberglass residue has been washed down the drain.

Avoid the natural inclination to rub dry fiberglass dust off the skin. Rubbing just forces it into the pores. A *cold* shower has proven the best way to remove fiberglass dust. Showering in hot water seems to open skin pores and allow dust to enter. Once glass dust gets into the skin, soap and water are useless. Follow cold water with a traditional warm shower. Don't expect miracles.

Many potentially toxic chemicals in paints and solvents can soak through ordinary clothing and into the skin. Du Pont makes disposable coveralls that are impervious to most paints, although epoxy resins seem to soak through. Look for these white suits at the local auto parts store. You may have to ask for them at the counter, as these suits are usually not displayed.

CHAPTER 2

TECHNIQUES

Repairing or installing new equipment on boats requires knowledge of various basic techniques. Bedding hardware and drilling holes in cored decks are two examples of techniques that are necessary to a variety of common jobs. This chapter is devoted to those general techniques that are called for in projects throughout the rest of the book.

BEDDING MATERIALS

Time: Five to ten minutes per piece of hardware.

Materials: Bedding compound, rags, solvent.

Tools: Putty knife, screwdriver, wrenches.

Safety: Skin protection when working with solvent.

Bedding is the term for the caulking or sealant used when installing deck hardware or other items that are screwed or bolted in place. It is also used on through-hull fittings, transducers, and other equipment mounted below the waterline. A variety of materials are used as bedding. Some are better above the waterline, while others are excellent for use underwater.

Oil-Based Bedding Compound: The oldest bedding material and still the least expensive, it is used between two pieces of wood or beneath hardware mounted on wood above the waterline. It is not used for mounting on fiberglass or metal. Clean up with mineral spirits. Working time indefinite. Produced only in "natural" color, it can be tinted with oil-based stains. Can be painted or varnished. Availability: pint and quart cans.

Silicone Rubber: Recommended for use only above the waterline, never below. Produces a watertight joint when properly used; can also be used to make custom gaskets in an emergency. Uncured silicone causes a mild skin reaction and has an ammonia-like aroma. It is not compatible with some plastics used in marine instruments. Produced in clear, white, black, and almond colors. Working time: 5 to 10 minutes. Wipe off uncured material with dry paper towels. Scrape or cut away cured materials. Clean tools with mineral spirits. Availability: tubes and cartridges.

Polysulfide Caulking: Produces a flexible bond that has good adhesion to wood, fiberglass, plastic, and metal. (May not be compatible with some plastics.) Joint can be taken apart with some effort. Excellent for use above waterline and good for use below. Clean up with mineral spirits. Produced in black, white, and mahogany colors. Working time: up to twenty-four hours.

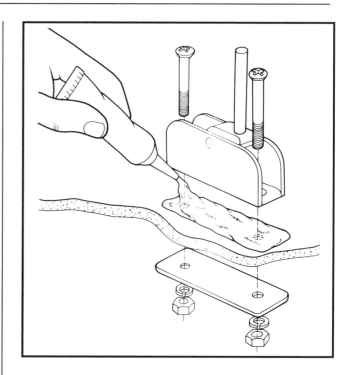

Bedding is applied between fittings and the deck to stop water leaks. The material can be applied either to the fitting or the deck, whichever is more convenient. Special attention should be paid to the bolt holes, which provide a handy path for water leaks. It's always better to use too much than too little bedding. Excess bedding should always squeeze out when the bolts are tightened.

Cure time depends on moisture content of air. Cure can be hastened by wiping with damp rag. Availability: tubes and cartridges. Also available in professional, two-part packaging.

Polyurethane Adhesive/Sealer: Provides a flexible joint with astounding adhesive qualities. Once cured, it will be difficult or impossible to break the joint without damaging the mated materials. Recommended for use above or below the waterline on permanently installed items. Bonds to wood, plastic, fiberglass, and metal. A primer may be necessary on oily woods such as teak. Not recommended for use in teak-planked decks, as polyurethane sealers are not compatible with many teak cleaners. Clean up with special solvents or mineral spirits. Produced in white, tan, and mahogany colors. Availability: tubes and cartridges.

Bedding keeps water from getting between the fitting and the deck. This is critical on wooden decks where a "water sandwich" can be the start of dreaded dry rot. Bedding hardware also stops water from seeping down mounting bolts and into either the core material of the deck or the interior of the boat. Water entering around deck-hardware mounting bolts is a key factor in the failure of balsa (and other) cored decks. Sealing hardware also prevents the nuisance of water dripping from mounting bolts onto sleeping crew members.

Below the waterline, the overriding reason for bedding through-hull fittings is to prevent sinking. Any hole in the hull is an open invitation to the sea. The deeper the fitting lies below the waterline, the more pressure behind the water that is trying to find a way into the boat.

Choosing the Right Compound

The choice of bedding compound depends on the nature of the job and personal preference. Oil-based bedding compound should be used on wooden-boat deck hardware. Silicone is best for hardware that needs to be removed at regular intervals. One-part polysulfide caulk makes sense above the waterline on fiberglass boats because it makes a long-lasting seal that can be broken relatively easily. Below the waterline, polyure-thane adhesive/sealant is best because its strong adhesive qualities are well suited to sea cocks, transducers, and other pieces of hardware that are seldom removed from the hull.

Avoid Dry Joints

Leaks around hardware (above or below the waterline) are primarily the result of "dry" joints. A dry joint results when either not enough bedding was used or all of the bedding was squeezed out when the bolts were tightened. There are plenty of cracks and crevices through which water can find its way into the boat. Sometimes, though less frequently, bedding failures occur because the surfaces were not properly prepared or the wrong materials were used.

A critical first step when bedding hardware is to get the base of the fitting and the mating surface squeaky clean. Dirt or old, dry compound will prevent good adhesion of the best compound. All traces of solvent or water used for cleaning should be eliminated before starting the job.

There is no advantage to scrimping on bedding. Use it liberally and joints won't leak. Run a generous bead around the bottom of all hardware, and put an additional "doughnut" around bolt holes. Covering the entire base of the fitting isn't being wasteful. For good measure, squirt some sealant into the actual holes in the deck. Remember, the goal is to seal both the piece of hardware and the bolt holes. Think like a drop of water. Try to imagine and block every possible pathway that water might follow into the boat.

Silicone products are particularly susceptible to dry joints caused by tightening bolts too soon after installing the hardware. When using silicone, tighten bolts only until goo starts to ooze out from beneath the fitting. Put aside the wrench and kick back with a cool one; let the silicone "set" for at least the time it takes to drink a can of Dr Pepper. Once the silicone partially cures, you are far less likely to squeeze the joint dry while tightening the bolts. Let the squeezin's around the base of the fitting cure before cutting them away with a sharp knife.

Polyurethane and polysulfide sealants are easy to clean off fiberglass or varnished wood before they are cured. Cut a small scrap of clean cardboard to use as a palette. Pick up the biggest gobs with a putty knife and wipe them onto the cardboard. (Keep the excess sealant clean and use it quickly to bed another fitting.) Follow with a rag wetted with the suggested solvent for the compound being used, or with ordinary mineral spirits. Turn the rag often and discard it when it becomes saturated with sealant. Wear rubber gloves to keep hands clean and protect skin. Once they are cured, removing either of these caulkings is difficult.

Special cleaners are now available for polyurethane sealants. Instead of harsh chemicals, these cleaners are citrus-based (yes, as in citrus fruit). They come in two varieties, one with skin softeners and one without. Sika's SSR is one example.

LEARNING ABOUT EPOXY

Time: Varies with job. Epoxy cure time varies from five minutes to several hours.

Materials: Epoxy resin, hardener, mixing cup, mixing stick, solvent.

Tools: Putty knife, paint brush, paint roller, glue syringe.

Safety: Always avoid getting epoxy resin or hardener on the skin. Gloves are recommended. Use eye protection when mixing or spreading mixed epoxy.

Perhaps the most useful materials available to the amateur are epoxy resins. These can be used to glue wood, to fair lead sailboat keels, and to make major repairs on fiberglass boats. At least a half-dozen companies make quality products. The materials produced by two of these companies have become universal boatyard standards: WEST System and Marine-Tex. The ubiquitousness of these products justifies recommending them by name for certain jobs, although equivalent products may be available in various localities and may be substituted.

WEST System

WEST System products are manufactured by the Gougeon Brothers, Inc., of Bay City, Michigan. As their name suggests, they comprise a system that

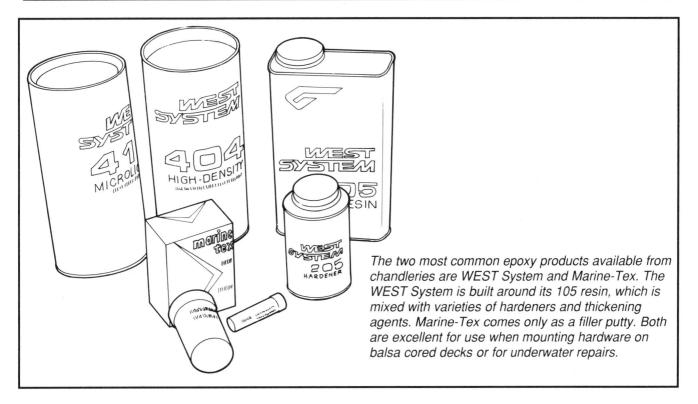

The two most common epoxy products available from chandleries are WEST System and Marine-Tex. The WEST System is built around its 105 resin, which is mixed with varieties of hardeners and thickening agents. Marine-Tex comes only as a filler putty. Both are excellent for use when mounting hardware on balsa cored decks or for underwater repairs.

includes a variety of resins, hardeners, fillers, additives, and a special solvent. The "heart" of the system is the company's 105 epoxy resin. This slightly pale amber, low-viscosity epoxy resin is designed to wet out and bond with wood fiber, fiberglass, and a variety of metals. An excellent adhesive, it will fill gaps and bridge voids when modified with fillers. It can be sanded and shaped when cured. WEST System 105 resin is mixed with any of four special hardeners, depending upon the working conditions or desired properties of the cured resin:

Like all epoxy resins, those of the WEST System must be mixed in exactly the correct proportions with hardener. This ratio is specified for each product. Unlike with polyester resins, the curing of epoxies cannot be "promoted" by adding extra hardener. Instead of speeding up the cure, extra hardener just weakens the final hardened epoxy. There's a long chemical explanation, but tests show that the characteristics of epoxies are significantly degraded by an improper resin-to-hardener ratio.

Improper mixing is the number-one cause of epoxy failure. Unmixed resin or hardener will remain a sticky liquid forever, even trapped inside a "bubble" of cured epoxy. Professionals working with epoxy resins know the importance of proper mixing and will spend several minutes stirring resin and hardener to insure a uniform batch.

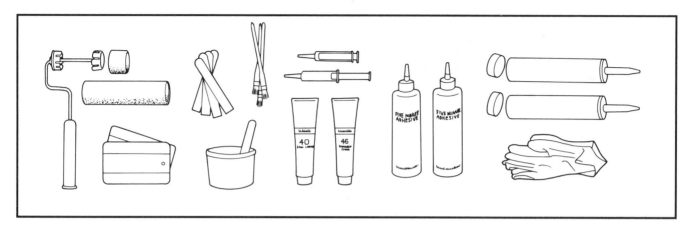

The tools that are commonly used for applying epoxy products include: small, metal-handled, disposable brushes; wooden stirring sticks; syringes for injecting resin; plastic mixing containers; plastic "squeegee" spreaders for smoothing putty; and a foam roller cover on a standard paint roller frame. Disposable rubber gloves or a protective skin cream should be used to avoid skin allergic reactions. Epoxy materials can be put into empty caulking tubes for filling seams or cracks.

Flexible plastic bowls such as those that margarine is packaged in make excellent mixing containers for epoxy resins. Shape the mixing stick to fit into the radius of the corner between the side and the bottom of the bowl. When the job is done, forget about cleaning the mixing bowl until the epoxy has fully cured. Bending the plastic sides will crack the epoxy out of the bowl and allow it to be discarded. The bowl will be clean enough for another job.

A variety of agents can be used to thicken mixed epoxy resin into a paste or putty-like consistency. The WEST System offers a variety of high- and low-density fillers specifically designed for this purpose. In general, high-density fillers make a thicker paste but are harder to sand. Low-density fillers sand more easily, but more filler is needed to achieve a pastelike consistency. Sanding dust and fine sawdust can also be used to thicken epoxies when gluing or fairing wood.

Epoxy resins can form excellent secondary bonds to cured polyester such as is used in fiberglass boats. In fact, epoxies bond better to cured polyester than does fresh polyester resin. This is why epoxies are rapidly becoming the standard repair materials in the fiberglass boat business. Epoxy resins can be applied with brushes, with paint rollers, or injected with syringes. Thickened epoxy is normally applied with a putty knife.

Marine-Tex

Marine-Tex is an epoxy putty designed primarily for use as a filler or fairing compound. It can also be used as a bonding agent under some circumstances. Marine-Tex is supplied in kits of various sizes, which allows easy purchase of just enough material for a single job. It comes as two parts: a prethickened paste resin, and a liquid hardener.

WEST SYSTEM HARDENERS

Hardener	Description
205 Hardener	Used in the majority of situations for strength and moisture resistance. Pot life: nine to twelve minutes.
206 Slow Hardener	Used when extended working or curing time is desired. Also used at higher temperatures. Pot life: twenty to twenty-five minutes.
207 Special Coating Hardener	Used when an exceptionally clear, moisture-resistant natural wood finish is desired. Pot life: twenty to twenty-five minutes.
209 Special Tropical Hardener	For coating and/or bonding under extremely warm or humid conditions or when extended working is desired. Pot life: forty to fifty minutes.

Table 2.1

The two parts are premeasured; mixing them together starts the chemical reaction. Smaller batches can be mixed, but great care is necessary to insure that the proper amount of hardener is used.

Once cured, Marine-Tex sands well, although not without some effort. It makes an excellent substrate for overspraying with color-matched gel coat. Paint adheres well to this product, making it ideal for repairs to underwater portions of the hull.

MAKING HOLES IN BALSA CORED DECKS

> **Time:** Fifteen to twenty minutes per hole, plus epoxy cure time.
> **Materials:** Marine-Tex or similar epoxy mending putty, rags, acetone.
> **Tools:** Drill motor, drill bits, putty knife, mixing cup, small screwdrivers, shop vacuum, duct tape.
> **Safety:** Eye protection while drilling, skin protection while using epoxy putty and acetone.

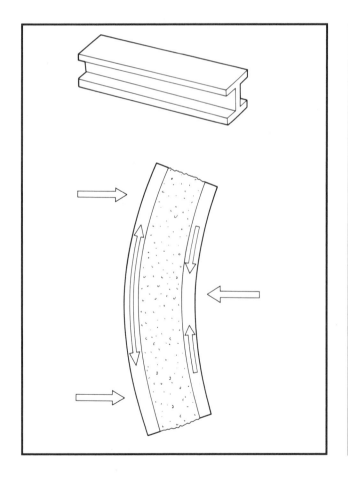

Modern cored fiberglass construction works on the same mechanical principle as a steel I-beam. The two skins of the fiberglass "sandwich" are held a specific distance apart just like the top and bottom plates of the beam. Like the webbing of the I-beam, the core serves only as a nonstructural spacer. Any load on the "sandwich" is opposed by the tensile properties of one skin and the compressive properties of the other. Problems arise when water causes the core material to decay.

Cored decks combine low weight with exceptional strength. Surprisingly, the cores are usually the same soft balsa wood that model airplane builders use. A balsa cored deck gets its strength not from the wood but because its construction is structurally analogous to a steel I-beam. Steel beams get their strength from the separation of their top and bottom plates. When an I-beam bends, the top plate must stretch while the bottom must compress. Since neither plate wants to get longer or shorter, the beam resists bending.

In a cored deck, one fiberglass skin must stretch while the other compresses if the deck is to bend.

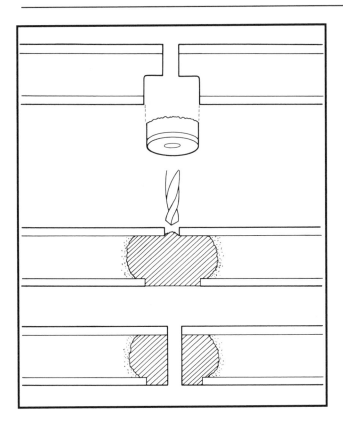

Mounting hardware on a balsa cored deck is a multi-step process. First, a hole the size of the mounting bolts is drilled from the outside. From underneath, a larger hole is created through the inner fiberglass skin only. The balsa core is then cut back to create a donut-shaped void around the hole. Epoxy putty is forced into the void and allowed to harden before the bolt hole is redrilled to size. The hardened epoxy prevents water from entering the balsa core and provides crush resistance against torque on the mounting bolts.

Just as with a steel I-beam, the strength comes from the resistance of the top and bottom plates (skins in the case of a cored deck) to stretching and compressing.

In an I-beam, the vertical webbing serves only to separate the top and bottom plates. Called the "webbing," much of it can be cut away to lighten the beam. The balsa wood, or closed-cell foam, in a boat deck serves the same function as webbing; it separates the fiberglass skins without providing any appreciable strength of its own. Balsa is chosen because of its light weight and low cost. Closed-cell plastic cores can be equally lightweight but are more expensive. Cored decks weigh only a fraction of conventional decks yet provide equal or greater strength.

Cored Deck Problems

Cored decks are fine until the time comes to attach a new piece of hardware. Then, soft balsa wood or crushable plastic foam becomes a problem. If holes are drilled through the core, tightening the nuts on the mounting bolts will crush the core and significantly weaken the deck. Even a large backing block on the inside doesn't eliminate the possibility of crushing the core.

Rot may be a serious problem with balsa cored decks. Bolt holes can never be trusted to be waterproof, no matter how well caulked. Water leaking into the core will inevitably cause balsa to soften and rot. This happens even with end-grain balsa, although the orientation of the grain greatly inhibits the spread of the damage.

Preparing the Deck

Mounting hardware on a balsa cored deck involves building a noncrushable epoxy tube around each bolt hole. This tube does two things: It seals the core against water and protects the balsa against being crushed when the mounting hardware is tightened. An appropriate putty can be made from thickened epoxy resin; or use Marine-Tex, a commercially prepared epoxy putty marketed in small kits perfect for mounting one or two items.

Mark the location of the new hardware on the deck with a soft pencil. Then go below to make sure the location of the bolt holes will be accessible from inside. Don't put a bolt somewhere it can't be reached with a washer and nut. Measure twice, just to be sure. Drill pilot holes with a small-diameter bit to double-check interior accessibility. These small holes are easily filled if a mistake has been made. Full-size bolt holes are drilled from the outside using these pilot holes as a guide.

The base of the piece of hardware can be used as a template. Drill one hole and drop a bolt through to hold the fitting while the second hole is drilled. Drop another bolt to hold alignment while the rest of the holes are drilled. This drilling technique avoids misalignment problems between the holes in the hardware and the holes in the deck. Use care to avoid enlarging the mounting holes in the fitting while drilling.

Remove the fitting and the bolts before going below to work from underneath. Enlarge the holes through just the inner skin by approximately ½ inch in diameter. A speed bore or small hole saw will do the job. Have a helper hold the suction nozzle of a vacuum cleaner just below where the drill is cutting into the fiberglass; this will suck up 90 percent of the dust and chips.

Do **not** enlarge the holes through the outer skin of the cored deck. The outer holes must remain the correct size for the mounting bolts. Enlarge only the holes in the inner skin. Once they are en-larged, use a miniature screwdriver or small chisel to dig out the balsa core from around the inner holes. Dig back at least ¼ inch from the edge of the inner hole. Some raggedness in the balsa is acceptable since it will never be seen again. Use a vacuum to clean up any chips and to clear the hole of balsa "fuzz."

Mix the Marine-Tex or epoxy putty according to instructions. It should be the consistency of cold peanut butter. Trowel this putty into the groove between the two laminates. A flat-blade electrician's screwdriver is just about perfect for forcing the putty deep into the recess between the upper and lower deck skins. Once the groove is filled, put a piece of duct tape over the inside hole. Go outside and push putty into the bolt hole until the entire cavity is filled except for a small dimple indicating the center of the bolt hole. The tape inside keeps the putty from sagging out of the hole while it cures. Clean tools with acetone on a rag.

Allow enough time for the epoxy putty to set up before peeling the duct tape off the inside. Working from the outside, redrill the holes with a twist drill of the appropriate size for the bolts. Have someone hold a coffee can under each hole to catch the drillings. Being neat in the first place is easier than cleaning up at the end of the job.

Use a flashlight to verify that the sides of the new holes are smooth, with no cracks or fissures through which water might seep into the balsa core. Re-epoxy any bad holes. If the holes are okay, mount the piece of hardware in the conventional manner using bedding, through bolts, backing plates, and self-locking nuts. (See the section on "Bedding Materials" on page 17.)

This technique works well on decks and other areas above the waterline. Balsa cored hulls need special attention from professionals.

CUTTING LARGE HOLES

Time: Ten minutes.

Materials: None.

Tools: ⅜-inch drill motor, pilot drill bit, hole saw.

Safety: Electric tool safety.

Installing new sea cocks or depth sounder transducers involves cutting rather large holes in the hull. A powerful electric drill motor (⅜-inch chuck and 4-amp motor or larger) fitted with a hole saw is required. Operating such a large, unwieldy tool in the cramped confines of a boat bilge is nearly impossible, but drilling a big hole from the outside invites disaster, since bulkheads and other structural members are hidden from view.

Instead of starting with a hole saw from the outside, drill a small pilot hole through the hull from *inside* the boat. A ³⁄₁₆-inch bit in a manual (or battery-powered) drill works well because it fits the confined spaces inside the boat. Pick the location for this guide hole well clear of any bulkheads or other potential obstructions. Again, measure twice before drilling, then check the measurements again. If a mistake is made, the resulting small hole is easy to plug with epoxy putty.

Have a helper outside the boat near where the hole will be located. Run the drill bit through the hull and hold it there until the helper finds it and marks the hole with a yellow lumber crayon. The bright yellow mark helps avoid the "Where the hell's the hole?" routine. Set up a ⅜-inch corded electric drill motor with an appropriate-size hole saw outside the boat where there is plenty of room to work.

HOLE SAW–BUYING TIPS

Use the best hole saw available. Good hole saws are made out of a single piece of steel that rings like a bell when struck. Each saw cuts a specific size hole. They mount on mandrels, which, in turn, mount on a ¼-inch drill bit. The mandrel almost never wears out, but expect to replace drill bits occasionally and saws more often, as grinding through fiberglass dulls the teeth.

The pilot hole guides the drill bit of the hole saw. Use light, even pressure to keep the round saw blade flat in its circular groove so that as many saw teeth as possible are cutting. Don't "rock" the saw from side to side. Rocking causes the blade to bind in the hole, so it actually takes longer to cut

A ⅜-inch electric drill motor can spin a hole saw up to 3 inches in diameter. Both hands are needed to control the torque of the motor. Hold the saw so that all of the teeth cut simultaneously in the circular groove. Constant pressure is needed, but avoid causing the motor to bog down or overheat. It can take several minutes to cut through a thick hull. Expect the saw to be hot enough to burn your skin once the hole is cut.

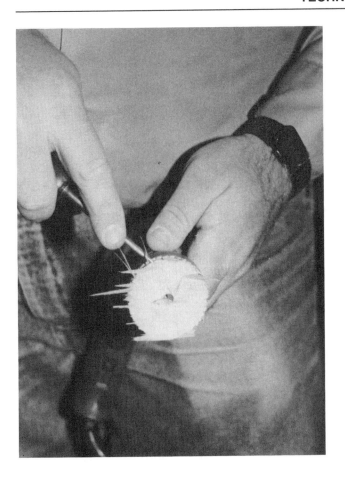

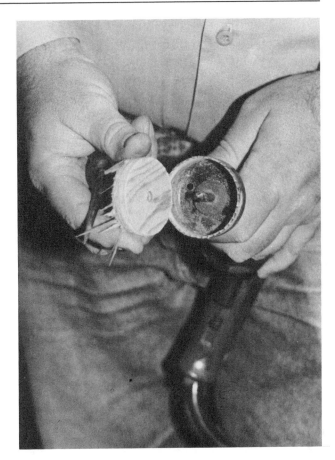

Removing the core from the hole saw can be irksome. An awl can be used to prize the plug out. Some saws have slots that allow the use of a screwdriver to push out the plug. Removing the pilot bit may be necessary to loosen a particularly stubborn core. After you have removed it from the saw, keep the core as a sample of hull or bulkhead.

the hole. Also, don't be tempted to "crowd" the drill motor to get the job done in a hurry. Spinning a hole saw is harder work than most motors want to do: Pushing too hard will cause the motor to overheat and eventually burn out.

Expect the hole saw to pop out the other side once it cuts through the hull. Let rotation stop before withdrawing it back outside. Resist any temptation to touch that hole saw; it will be extremely hot. Let the saw cool for at least five minutes before attempting to extract the plug of fiberglass that is stuck inside.

Removing the plug is just a matter of easing it out with a screwdriver through the slots in the sides of the saw. Smaller saws do not have slots. They require the use of an awl to loosen the plug. If the plug is really stuck, try sliding the ¼-inch pilot bit out of the mandrel. This may allow enough "play" for the plug to pop out more easily.

AVOID OVERHEATING TOOLS

Electric drill motors and other electric tools can be damaged by overheating. Help them stay cool by keeping the speed of the motor high so that its built-in fan blows plenty of cooling air over the armature. If the motor still gets hot, pull the tool out of the work and let the motor run at full speed with no load for a minute or so. High-speed running pushes a lot of cooling air through the motor, so it cools faster than if it were just shut off.

The dead giveaway of an overheating tool is a "hot electrical" smell. There may also be excessive sparking inside the motor housing. Once hot solder and bits of metal start to spit out of the motor, fatal damage has been done.

CORRECT SIZE HOLES FOR SCREWS

Time: Under one minute.

Materials: None.

Tools: Drill motor, twist drills.

Safety: Electric tool safety.

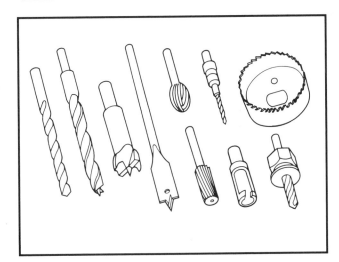

An assortment of drill bits is needed for either a corded or battery-powered electric drill motor. Standard twist drills are suitable for making holes in wood, fiberglass, or metal. Brad-point wood bores, forstner bits, and spade bores can be used only in wood. Tapered wood-screw bits and plug (bung) cutters are also woodworking tools. The mandrel and hole saw can be used in wood or fiberglass, although cutting fiberglass rapidly dulls its teeth. Burrs are primarily for metalworking, but they prove useful for enlarging or "customizing" holes in wood and fiberglass.

Somebody should invent portable holes that could be slapped down wherever one is needed. A really good portable hole could be peeled up and used over and over again. Until this improbable invention comes along, holes will have to be drilled when mounting hardware. The importance of holes is often overlooked because they don't show when the job is done. (Or, they shouldn't show.) However, the long-term quality of the finished job is often determined by the skill with which the holes were made.

Boats are always subject to vibration and strain. Fasteners mounted in holes drilled too large can never be properly tightened. As a result, normal vibration quickly loosens joints. The first obvious sign that something is wrong is slight movement of the parts under load. A bit later on, there will be constant wiggling. Eventually, things fall apart.

It is virtually impossible to drill a hole that is too small for a fastener without noticing the problem. An undersize hole for a wood screw results in splitting the wood. In fiberglass, a hole that's too small for a self-tapping screw causes the screw head to snap off when it's tightened. Bolts, of course, just won't go into holes smaller than their diameter.

Wood Screws

A wood screw works by wedging itself into the fibers of the wood. This wedging action exerts a considerable outward pressure that will crack or split the wood unless a pilot hole has been drilled. The best wood-screw pilot holes are made with tapered drill bits that match the taper of the screw (that is, use a number 8 bit for a number 8 screw). Tapered pilot bits are available from stores catering to serious woodworkers but are rare in neighborhood hardware stores.

Ordinary straight twist drills can be used to make wood-screw pilot holes. The drill must be small enough to allow maximum "bite" of the screw threads into the board. Oversize pilot holes result in loss of holding power. The following table lists starting points for choosing pilot drill sizes. You may have to increase or decrease the size of

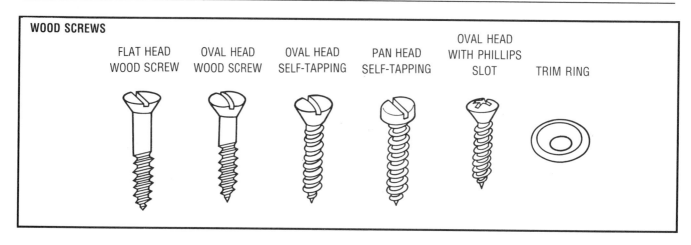

WOOD SCREWS

FLAT HEAD WOOD SCREW — OVAL HEAD WOOD SCREW — OVAL HEAD SELF-TAPPING — PAN HEAD SELF-TAPPING — OVAL HEAD WITH PHILLIPS SLOT — TRIM RING

the pilot hole, depending on the brand of screws, wood density, or other factors.

The depth of the pilot hole should be ⅛ inch shorter than the screw for sizes 8 and smaller. It should be ¼ inch shorter for sizes 10 and larger. When possible, drill test holes in scrap. Soft woods demand smaller pilot holes for adequate grip of the screw threads. Denser hardwoods require larger holes to prevent the screw from snapping. Note that a larger drill must be used to make the hole for the unthreaded shank than for the threaded portion of the screw.

A shallow countersunk recess is needed to allow oval head screws to lie flush with the surface of the wood. Special tools known as countersinks do this job properly. Most people cheat by using an ordinary twist drill slightly larger in diameter than the head of the screw. Drill only deep enough to create a "dish" that will accommodate the screw head.

WOOD SCREW PILOT HOLES
(in hardwoods)

Screw Size (number)	Shank Hole (in inches)	Pilot Hole (in inches)
4	3/64	5/64
6	1/16	3/32
8	11/64	7/64
10	3/16	1/8
12	7/32	9/64
14	1/4	3/16

Table 2.2

Self-Tapping Screws

Self-tapping screws (also known as "sheet-metal screws") are popular in boat construction. Stainless-steel self-tappers have replaced bronze wood screws because of their lower cost and greater availability. Self-tappers hold in wood, metal, or fiberglass. The size of pilot holes required depends on the material into which the screws are being fastened.

When using self-tapping screws, let the threads do the work, not the shank or body of the screw. In most cases, the pilot hole diameter should equal, or very slightly *exceed*, the diameter of the shank. The only exception is soft wood where the wedging action of the shank adds to the screw's holding ability. In metal, the pilot hole must be slightly larger than the diameter of the shank.

Fiberglass adds complications. The threads of self-tapping screws actually loosen individual glass fibers in the laminate. This means that the diameter of the pilot hole effectively gets smaller as the screw is driven home. The result can be disastrous if a large enough pilot hole was not drilled in the first place. The screw will turn easily at the beginning. Each turn chews more glass fibers into the hole and more effort will be required. Finally, so much effort will be needed that the screw snaps.

The following table should be used as a guide, but cannot be taken as gospel in every case. Testing or experimentation may be needed to determine the correct pilot hole for any given situation. As a rule, self-tappers in fiberglass need a larger pilot hole than in metal.

Stainless-steel self-tapping screws come in three types of heads: The *pan head* is a flat, round disk on top of the threaded portion. Nearly all pan heads have a straight slot for an ordinary screwdriver. Pan heads lie proud on the surface when the screw is tight. Pan head screws are often used

SELF-TAPPING SCREW PILOT HOLES (in thin metal)

Screw Size (number)	Pilot Hole (in inches)
4	3/32
6	7/64
8	1/8
10	9/64
12	5/32

Table 2.3

to join fiberglass pieces together, like a deck to its hull. There is little use for pan head screws in woodworking.

Flat head stainless self-tappers are hard to find. More common are *oval head* screws. An oval head requires a countersink like a wood screw, but the top of the head is not flat. Instead, it bulges up like a small dome. This design allows deeper slots in the head so that the screwdriver is less likely to slip out when tightening the screw. Nearly all oval heads are cut for Phillips screwdrivers. Oval head screws look fine when simply recessed into the wood; the addition of a "trim ring" (also known as a "finishing washer") gives a professionally finished appearance. Trim rings are sized to match specific size screws. (Use a number 10 trim ring for a number 10 screw, and so on.)

Bolt Holes

The rule of thumb with bolts is to drill the holes exactly the same size as the bolt. Undersize holes require force to drive the bolt through, damaging either the material surrounding the hole or the bolt threads. Oversize holes allow for "slop" in the fastener, which leads to gradual joint failure. There is one exception to making holes exactly the right diameter: Bolt holes in soft wood can be slightly smaller than the bolt since the bolt can be driven through with a nonmetallic hammer. (A 16-ounce framing hammer will destroy the head.)

PRO TIP: TIGHT WOOD SCREWS

It's not uncommon for screws to bind when being driven into hard wood. Dick Minier, who learned his craft at the Matthews Boat Company during its heyday, uses beeswax as a lubricant instead of soap. He heats the beeswax in a double boiler (being very careful of fire) and then dips the tips of the screws into the molten wax. The wax is allowed to harden before using the screws. Beeswax lubricates the threads enough to ease the effort necessary to drive them into harder woods.

Ordinary bar soap is often promoted as a screw lubricant. It works well in home woodworking but can cause problems in the dampness around boats. Soap is caustic. Eventually it causes a screw to "freeze" in the hole. Years later, it's almost impossible to remove the screw because of the action of the soap.

HIDING SCREW HOLES WITH WOOD BUNGS

Time: Five minutes per plug, plus setting time of glue.

Materials: Wooden plugs, glue, sandpaper, rags.

Tools: Installation: drill motor, combination pilot drill and countersink, plug cutter, chisel. Removal: hand-cranked drill, brad-point drill bit, awl.

Safety: Caution with sharp chisel. Plug cutter should be used in drill press or with drill motor in drill guide.

Nothing about a boat is more beautiful than bright, finished wood trim and interior furnishings. Constructing such items often calls for screws or other fasteners in the middle of an otherwise unblemished plank. The best way to hide screw heads is with a wooden plug of the same material as the plank. A properly installed bung becomes so much a part of the joiner work that it virtually disappears. Bungs have become the hallmarks of professional craftsmen, but the technique is simple enough to learn.

Cutting Bungs

This can be the easiest part of the job, since ready-made bungs are sold by most large chandleries. Usually called "plugs" in the stores, bungs are available in mahogany or teak in sizes of ⅜, ⁵⁄₁₆, ½, and ⅝ inch. Ready-made bungs are satisfactory for small jobs. But, if more than a half dozen or so are needed, it makes sense to cut them at home. Bungs cut from scrap wood taken from the job match the grain structure of the finished work much better than any store-bought bungs.

Plug-cutting tools are available in the same ⅜-, ½- and ⅝-inch sizes as ready-made bungs. These cutters are available individually, or you can save a few dollars by purchasing an entire set. Cutters should be used in a drill press because more control over the cutter is needed than is possible with a hand-held drill motor. (Note: Cutters are sold as "plug cutters" since that's what woodworkers call them. The term *bung* is used almost exclusively by boat builders.)

Find a piece of scrap wood from the job that is at least ½-inch thick. Tack the wood temporarily to another piece of scrap. Set the depth stop on the drill press so that the cutter just barely goes through the stock and into the scrap beneath. Then remove each bung from the cutter body before cutting the next one. See the instructions on the cutter for exact details.

Cut as many bungs as possible from the piece of scrap. Extra bungs are never really extra. They'll all be used eventually. Store loose bungs in a coffee can or plastic jar with a lid so that when it is knocked over, bungs don't spill into the bilge.

Drilling Bung Holes

Screws heads that will be bunged should be recessed a minimum of ⅛ inch below the surface. If ordinary twist drills are used, at least two are needed: one the diameter of the screw shank for the pilot hole, and the other the diameter of the screw head for the bung counterbore. Drilling twice is cumbersome and ordinary twist drills sometimes don't yield the perfectly round hole needed for a professional bunging job.

A better way is to use a combination pilot bit and counterbore. One operation creates the pilot hole for the screw and recesses the head for plugging. These are available in the same sizes as plug cutters and ready-made bungs. Look for tapered pilot bits because tapered pilot holes are best for wood screws. (Note: Always try to buy plug cutters and counterbores made by the same company. This assures a tight fit in the finished work.)

The depth of the pilot hole can be adjusted by moving the drill bit within the attached counterbore to match the length of the screws being used. Some counterbores also have an adjustable stop collar that controls depth. Depth stops are handy, but most workers can do an adequate job without them.

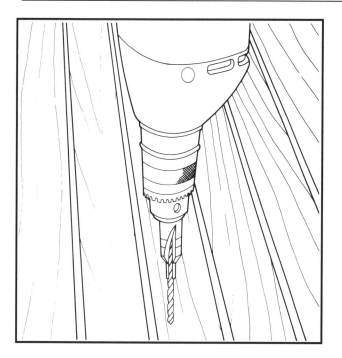

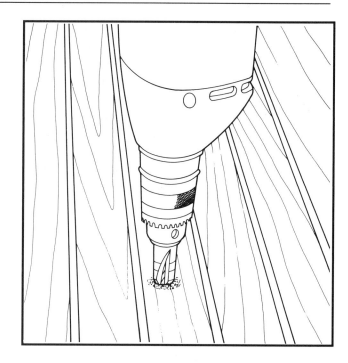

Start the screw hole using special combination pilot bit and counterbore wood bit. It is critical that the drill be held exactly at a right angle to the surface of the wood. The size of the pilot bit and counterbore is determined by the size of the wood screw to be installed.

Allow the shank of the combination pilot bit and counterbore to bite into the wood. This cuts the larger hole needed to recess the screw head beneath the wood bung. Depth of cut must be carefully controlled. The counterbore should never penetrate more than half the thickness of the wood.

Once the hole is drilled, screws are installed in the conventional manner. Be sure they are drawn tightly into the recess, but don't use so much force that the screwdriver jumps out of the slots and damages the side walls of the recess. Damaged counterbore walls make tight-fitting bungs impossible.

Professionals prefer oval head Phillips screws because they have more metal in the slots to prevent the screwdriver from slipping. Square drive screws work even better with power drivers but are hard to find in bronze or stainless steel.

Installing Bungs

Check each counterbore hole for traces of beeswax used to lubricate the screws. All wax must be removed for the glue to hold the bungs firmly. Mix an appropriate glue, such as resorcinol, urea-formaldehyde, or epoxy, in a small container (a clean tuna fish can will do). If a squeeze-bottle adhesive is being used, it helps to put the glue in a small, flat container. Use a small stick or a toothpick to rub glue into the countersunk recesses, being sure to get plenty of glue on the side walls.

Select bungs that match the coloring and grain structure of the work. Dip one end in the glue, then orient the grain of the bung so that it is parallel to the grain in the plank. Gently tap it into the countersunk hole. Some glue should ooze out around the bung, and the top of the plug should stand proud above the surface of the plank.

Tap bungs *gently*. Hard hammer blows will split the wood without actually driving the plug any deeper. It is not necessary to tap the bung all the way down until it jams against the screw. In fact, leaving a small gap between the bung and screw head allows for easier removal when that time comes.

Use a clean rag to wipe up any glue spills or globs oozing out around the bungs. Dip the rag in an appropriate solvent. It's a lot easier to clean up wet glue than to sand it off later after it dries and hardens. With cleanup done, go have lunch and then take time to sharpen your chisels on an oil stone. This allows the glue to set up in peace. Watched glue never sets.

Trimming Bungs

Beginners should let the glue harden completely before attempting to trim and sand the bungs. Experienced workers trim and sand the bungs of interior jobs while the water-based glue is still tacky. Sanding dust mixes into the glue, making an effective wood filler the exact color of the surrounding wood. This trick works with aliphatic and white wood glues only. Two-part epoxies and resorcinol glues lack the wet strength to allow trimming with

The wood screw is then driven home until its head is recessed in the counterbore. Note that the depth of the recess here is about 3/16 of an inch. A Phillips screw was chosen to allow use of an electric screwdriver.

a chisel until they have set to the "rubber" stage, when it's too late for the sanding dust to mix with the glue.

There is a knack to clipping off the tops of bungs. Place the chisel against the bung, then strike the chisel smartly. A quick, smart tap cuts cleanly. Always cut *with* the grain and trim about half the height of the bung at a time. Do not attempt to cut the bung flush with the first blow. This usually results in breaking the bung below the surface of the plank. Instead, take off thin "baloney slices" until it is almost flush.

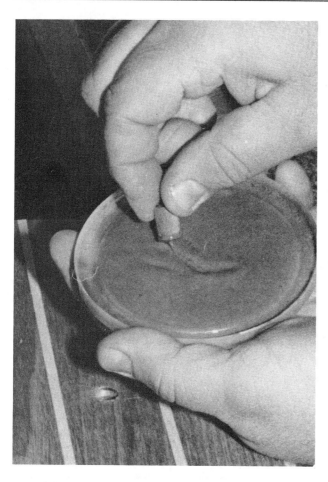

One end of the wood bung (plug) is rubbed in wood glue. It is important to get some glue on the sides of the bung. In this case, a plastic coffee can lid has been used to hold the glue, making it easy to dip the end and roll the sides in the glue.

After being dipped in glue, the wooden bung (plug) is inserted into the counterbore of the hole. It is important that the grain of the bung line up with the grain pattern of the wood. Improper grain alignment will cause the bung to stand out when the project is completed.

Use a hammer to gently tap the bung into the hole. Gently is the key word. Hard blows will damage the bung or the sides of the hole. Some excess glue should squeeze out around the bung.

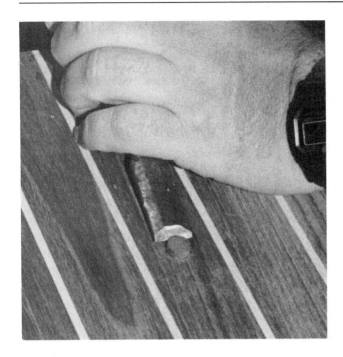

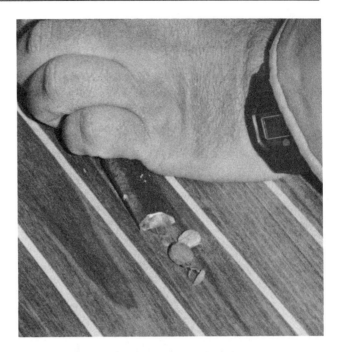

A sharp wood chisel is used to clip off the excess length of wood bung. The blade of the chisel should be held as close to horizontal as possible. Line up the chisel so that it cuts with the grain of the bung. Cutting across the grain will cause the bung to shatter instead of being clipped off cleanly.

Use a sharp chisel and apply small, light taps from a hammer to clip off thin slices of the bung. Excess force will either damage the bung or cause the chisel to dig into the surrounding wood. Make sure to hold the chisel in the position shown. Cutting several thin slices is better than trying to snip the bung off with one blow.

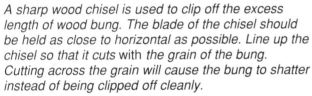

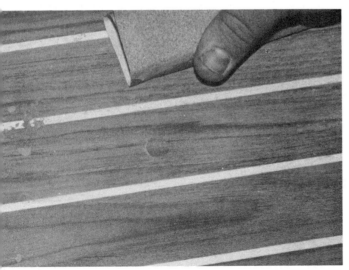

Use a wooden block and sandpaper to complete installation of the bung. When the plug is flush with the surrounding surface, it is then ready for final finishing. If conventional wood glue was used, the glue line will have picked up some sanding dust. This line will disappear once the glue dries.

A hammer can be used to strike the chisel at first, but put it away when the bung is less than ¹⁄₁₆ inch high. Do the rest by hand. Work with a chisel that is wider than the bung. Do not try to cut the bung absolutely flush with a chisel. That's a job for sandpaper. Wrap 100-grit sandpaper around a square stick to sand only the bung and not the wood around it until the bung is flush. Then finish-sand the entire area.

Leichtung Workshops offers a flush-cutting, off-set dovetail saw that can be used instead of cutting bungs with a chisel. The handle of this saw swivels to allow cutting left or right. This tool has only one drawback: It requires a relatively large, flat area in which to work. Confined spaces and unusual curves found on boats may prevent its use. (Available from Leichtung Workshops, 4944 Commerce Parkway, Cleveland, Ohio 44128. Ask for tool number 78287.)

Invariably, a bung or two breaks off below the surface of the surrounding plank. Even professionals experience this problem. The only solution is to remove the broken bung and replace it with a new one. There are no shortcuts or tricks. Removal and replacement may be tedious, but it's the only way.

Removing Wood Bungs

Removing wood bungs is time consuming, but if done right, the existing hole will be undamaged and ready for the installation of a new bung. Don't be in a rush to get the old one out. Some break out cleanly, while others require fifteen or twenty minutes to take out, one chip at a time. Bungs installed with conventional wood glues come out easiest. Those glued with two-part epoxy or resorcinol adhesives will fight to the death.

The conventional method of bung removal is to choose a drill bit at least ⅛ inch *smaller* in diam-

eter than the bung. Drill out the body of the bung, leaving a ring of old bung all around the new hole, but note: Do not use an electric drill motor! Drilling must stop as soon as the tip of the drill bit strikes the metal of the screw to prevent damaging the slot. Knowing when to stop is a matter of sensing the different "bite" of the drill bit as it changes from wood to metal. This is nearly impossible when using an electric drill motor.

Picking out the ring of old bung takes time. Use a sharp awl or narrow chisel to break apart the wood fibers and pull pieces out of the hole. Be extremely careful not to damage the top of the hole. This must remain perfectly round with a sharp edge if the new bung is to fit tightly. Blow the tiny wood chips out of the hole or use a battery-powered hand vacuum to suck them up. The vacuum gets chips out of the hole better and when the job's done, so is the cleanup.

Slots of bunged screws are always filled with old glue. If a screw is to be removed, use an awl to break the glue out. Another way to crack off old glue is to insert a screwdriver into the slot and tap it with a hammer. (Wear eye protection!) Once the glue is out of the slot, the screw can be removed. However, watch carefully as the top of the screw comes out of the counterbore recess. Don't let the edge of the screw catch the rim of the hole and damage the roundness of the counterbore.

CHOOSING AND USING WOOD GLUES

Time: n/a

Materials: Two-part epoxy, two-part resorcinol, aliphatic resin glue, or white wood glue.

Tools: Small stick or brush, cleanup rag, mixing cup.

Safety: Gloves for skin protection. Eye and fire protection when using acetone.

Two pieces of wood can be glued together so that the joint is stronger than the wood itself. Yet glue joint failures remain a major problem for amateurs. Actually, it is rarely the glue that fails. The real failure is almost always the wrong choice of glue or improper application of the glue. Three things are needed for a good joint: The glue has to be right; the mating surfaces must be correctly prepared; and the joint itself must be properly designed. This sounds complicated, but it boils down to common sense.

Glues work by bonding to the wood fibers. For this bond to work, the glue must penetrate beyond the surface of the wood into its cellular structure. Modern power tools (planers, saws, and some sanders) "case harden" the surface of the wood and prevent the glue from penetrating. Weak joints result. Light sanding of machine-hardened surfaces with 100-grit paper removes the case hardened outer surface so that a strong joint can be achieved.

Glue joints want to be thin, because thick joints tend to be brittle and crack easily. Achieving a thin joint means that the mating surfaces must be mirror images of each other and as smooth as possible. The nature of wood allows for very flat, smooth cuts to be made with the grain, but cuts across the grain are never as smooth. Joints made with end grain wood are not as strong as those in which the wood is cut along the grain.

Most boat woods glue well, especially mahogany. There are exceptions. White oak can be glued, but it is not porous enough to allow good glue penetration. Joints in white oak should always have mechanical fasteners (screws or bolts) in addition to glue. Natural oils in teak can prove troublesome. The only way to get a good bond with teak is to first remove these oils with a degreasing agent. As with oak, mechanical fasteners are recommended in teak.

Glue Choice

Aliphatic resin glue is a stronger and more water-resistant second cousin to white glue. Normally, it is a dark cream color, or a light yellow, and has the consistency of the best Vermont maple syrup. Like white glue, aliphatic resin glue cleans up with water before it dries. Both of these glues come in handy soft plastic bottles that make application easy.

Resorcinol glue is the time-honored boat building glue. It is sold in two parts: a powder, and a thick resin. The two parts are mixed together in a small plastic cup according to directions before being applied to the wood. *Epoxy glues* are also two-part mixtures, but both parts come as viscous liquids. Epoxies must be mixed either by weight or volume (check the label) and the ratio of resin to hardener is critical to the final bond.

Clamps Hold Wet Joints

Joints that are not also mechanically fastened should be clamped until the glue has cured ("dried"). Err on the side of clamping for too long instead of for too short a time. Instructions on the glue's packaging are the best guideline, but remember that temperature and humidity play big roles in the speed of curing. Tighten the clamps until glue squeezes out around the joint, but *don't overtighten the clamps!* Too much pressure can squeeze out most of the glue, causing a weak joint. A thin line of glue should be visible where the two pieces of wood meet.

Tight clamping is necessary with almost all glues except those in the epoxy family. With epoxies, clamps should be set only tight enough to produce a properly aligned final joint. Cured epoxy is stronger than the surrounding wood, so a thick glue line does not mean a weak joint. However, overtight clamps could squeeze out the resin, resulting in a decidedly weaker joint.

White glue and aliphatic resin glue squeezin's can be removed with a rag dipped in warm water. Wiping off resorcinol glue with a rag is possible, but it often results in staining the wood with this adhesive's dark color. Excess epoxy can be wiped up with a rag and acetone or special epoxy solvent. It's better, however, not to wipe off resorcinol or epoxy glues. Instead, let them set to a "rubber"

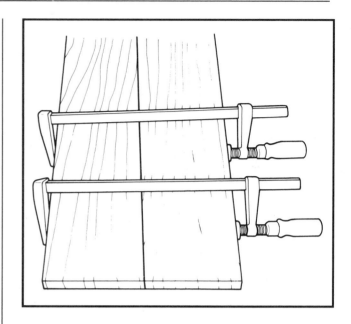

Clamps are used to hold glue joints while they dry. Careful alignment of the boards is necessary for a smooth joint. Equally important is the proper clamping pressure. Too much will cause a weak, "dry joint." Too little may result in an objectionable glue line. Several clamps should be used to disperse the pressure evenly along the joint. Avoid focusing it all in one place.

state. Then cut the rubbery glue away neatly with a sharp chisel.

Both the wood to be joined and the glue should be the same temperature. Many two-part glues (especially the epoxies) will work only at temperatures above 50 degrees. Curing times are heavily influenced by temperature, with cold weather slowing or altogether stopping the final cure. Heat lamps and small electric heaters can be used to warm small areas, so long as caution is taken to avoid overheating either the glue or the surrounding material. Hot temperatures can be deadly to fiberglass by causing the laminate to distort or actually come apart. Keep the heated surface below 85 degrees for safety.

Marine Glues

White Wood Glue (Carpenter's Glue): A favorite with shore-based cabinetmakers, this glue is neither water-resistant nor waterproof. It forms a semitransparent bond that hides well beneath stain or varnish, but it is *not recommended for marine use*.

Aliphatic Resin Glue: Often called "yellow carpenter's glue," this is high-tech white glue. Special resins give it better bonding qualities and it exhibits considerable water resistance, but it is not waterproof. The bond hides well beneath stain or varnish and can be tinted to match the wood. Packaged as thick, light-yellow liquid in a squeeze bottle.

Urea-Formaldehyde Resin Glues: These are one-part powders or two-part products consisting of a powder and a thick liquid. Once activated, a chemical reaction begins that cannot be stopped. Pot life is about an hour. Ad-

Table 2.4

WOOD GLUE SELECTION GUIDE	
Location	**Suggested Glues**
Exterior Teak (Unfinished or Oil Finish)	2-Part Epoxy or 2-Part Resorcinol
Exterior Wood (Varnished or Painted)	2-Part Epoxy or 2-Part Resorcinol or Urea-Formaldehyde Resin Glue
Interior Wood (Unfinished or Oiled)	Urea-Formaldehyde Resin Glue or Aliphatic Resin Glue
Interior Wood (Varnished)	Urea-Formaldehyde Resin Glue or Aliphatic Resin Glue or White Wood Glue
Note: Glues in each category are shown in descending order, with the best choice first.	

vantages include cleanup with water. Excess glue won't stain surrounding wood. Main disadvantage is that it does not fill gaps well. Bond is strong and extremely water-resistant.

Resorcinol Glues: They come in two parts that must be mixed together. Once activated, resorcinol glues have a pot life of thirty minutes to five hours, depending on brand and conditions. Resorcinol glues are probably the most cost-effective marine glues on the market. Bonds equal more expensive epoxies in terms of durability and holding strength. These glues have a decided reddish-brown color that blends well with mahogany but may produce a visible glue line in other woods. Glue spills can stain permanently. Cleanup is with plain water. Cured resorcinol glue is virtually unaffected by immersion in water.

Epoxy Glues: They come in two parts that must be mixed together. Accurate mixing is critical to final bond strength. Pot life of one to four hours, although concentrated amounts in small containers may "kick" unexpectedly, producing large amounts of heat. Setting time varies from a few hours to days, depending on brand and conditions. Cleanup of uncured epoxy is done with acetone.

Acrylic Resin Glue: An expensive two-part glue with a setting time of about five minutes. This glue will stick to almost everything and is waterproof, making it ideal for difficult repair jobs.

Wood glues are not intended to bond metal, plastic, or any materials other than wood. These materials require the use of a polyurethane adhesive-sealer.

SANDING WOOD AND FIBERGLASS

Time: Varies.

Materials: Sandpaper, sanding discs, bronze wool, rags.

Tools: Power sanders, sanding block, knife, shop vacuum.

Safety: Dust mask or respirator, hand protection, eye protection.

A couple of centuries ago, woodworkers smoothed the surface of a plank by grabbing a handful of beach sand and rubbing away. Since then the materials have improved, but the process remains basically the same. Modern sandpaper is just grains of sand (or some other cutting agent) glued to a paper backing. The paper makes handling the sand easier, but the cutting and smoothing action is pretty much identical to the handful-of-sand approach.

Two factors have to be considered in choosing sandpaper: the type of abrasive material, and the weight and type of backing paper. Flint quartz is the oldest abrasive. It has the singular advantage of being cheap, but it does not last very long in service. Aluminum oxide is slightly more expensive, but the cost is offset by improved machine or hand sanding. This type of paper is probably the best all-around buy. Garnet paper is the most expensive abrasive commonly available. It is an excellent choice for fine finishes. Other "sandpapers" use silicon carbide, emery, and crocus as abrasives primarily for metal finishing.

Abrasives are available in a range of grits from coarse to fine; micro-fine grits are available in some types of man-made abrasives. Since one manufacturer's definition of *fine* may be another's definition of *medium*, a system of numbers was developed to compare grits. The lower the number, the coarser the grit. In general, grits from 40 to 220 are used for finishing raw wood. Grits from 150 to 220 are used to sand between coats of paint or varnish. Anything above 220 is generally reserved for wet sanding painted coatings or gel coats.

Although the sizes of the abrasive particles are identical on papers of the same number, remember that each abrasive cuts differently. An aluminum oxide paper cuts faster than an equivalent flint quartz. Likewise, manufacturers often treat the abrasive material with a chemical coating to improve performance. Zinc stearate, which prevents sanding dust from clogging the abrasive, is one such coating. A zinc stearate–coated paper cuts faster than an uncoated paper of the same abrasive.

Sandpaper is sold in standard 9" x 11" sheets. Single sheets are available from most hardware stores, but buying a sleeve of a hundred sheets gets you a much better price per sheet. Avoid the "home handyman" packages sold by discount stores, as these are usually more expensive than purchasing an equivalent number of individual sheets. Standard sheets may be cut into quarters

Common Sandpaper Abrasives

Flint Quartz: Low cost, but wears away quickly. Best for hand sanding. Particles look like grains of sand, which they are.

Aluminum Oxide: Moderate cost; works well for hand sanding or with power sanders. Long cutting life.

Garnet: Easily identified by distinctive red color of abrasive. Favored for fine wood finishes.

Silicon Carbide (Carborundum): Extremely sharp particles that refracture in use so that new, sharp edges are constantly being produced. Good for fast sanding of wood or finishing metals.

SANDPAPER GRITS

Grit (number)	Description	Typical Use
20	Very Coarse	Fast cutting or shaping
40	Coarse	Fast cutting or shaping
60–80	Medium	Rough sanding or shaping
100–150	Fine	Intermediate sanding of mahogany; final sanding of teak
180–220	Very Fine	Finish sanding mahogany; dry sanding between coats of paint or varnish
220–280	Extra Fine	Dry sanding between coats of paint or varnish; wet sanding of coatings and gel coats
400–1,500	Super Fine	Wet sanding coatings or gel coats

Table 2.5

or thirds to fit power sanders; precut paper for power tools is considerably more expensive than purchasing standard sheets and cutting them.

Sheet sandpaper is sold in a variety of paper-backing weights, from light to heavy. The scale runs from "A" paper at the light end to "F" at the industrial-strength end. As a rule, "A" backing is best suited for finish sanding by hand while "C" or "D" weights are good for rough sanding or use with power tools. Some backings are impervious to water while others are not; waterproof backing is necessary for wet sanding.

Sandpaper is also manufactured in disks and belts for power tools. Sanding disks with self-stick backing are available in 5- to 8-inch diameters. Auto parts stores that stock automotive paints are the best sources for self-stick disks. Buy 'em by the box for the best price. Hardware stores stock the common sizes and grits of sanding belts. Disks are graded by the same grit numbers as sheets; sanding belts, however, often have only a verbal description, such as "fine," "medium," or "coarse."

New on the amateur market is 3M's Stikit. This

is a roll of adhesive-backed sandpaper the right width for quarter-sheet power sanders. Stikit requires a special pad on the sander, but otherwise is identical to ordinary sandpaper of equivalent grit. The manufacturer also offers a special dispenser that allows you to tear off exactly the amount of Stikit paper you need in much the same way as tearing off a paper towel.

Sanding Wood

There are two basic instructions for sanding wood. First, always work up through the grits. Rough sand and shape with 60 or 80 grit before moving to 120 for intermediate sanding. Final sanding is typically done with 180 grit before the first coat of paint or varnish is applied. Extremely hard woods may benefit from a final sanding with 220, but on soft or coarse woods this is a waste of time. Teak should not be sanded beyond 80 grit if it will get an oil or varnish finish. Fine sandpaper gives a smooth, burnished surface to teak that is almost impervious to protective oil coatings.

The second basic sanding instruction is to *always* work *with* the grain. Sandpaper wears millions of small scratches in the surface of the wood. The finer the paper, the smaller the scratches until they blend together into what appears to be a smooth surface. Some scratches from the coarse paper always remain after finish sanding. If they run with the grain, they remain hidden by the natural appearance of the wood grain.

Scratches across the grain are actually highlighted by the natural structure of the wood. The eye spots them immediately because they run at 90 degrees to the grain pattern. Even if the damage is not immediately visible it can still cause problems. Cross-grain scratches caused by sanding always show up prominently when stain or varnish is applied.

Hand sanding should almost always be done with a sanding block. It is virtually impossible to sand a flat surface with just paper in bare hands because human fingers cannot give the even support of a sanding block. Scrap two-by-four stud makes an excellent sanding block because of its rounded edges. Fold the paper around the wood and go to work. To make the ultimate sanding block, glue a piece of thin felt to the working side of the block.

Makita, Milwaukee, Black & Decker, and Porter-Cable all offer excellent electric sanding machines. *Palm sanders* and *reciprocating sanders* do the same job, but there is an important difference: the motion of the sanding pad. The pad of a palm sander actually moves in a random orbit. Cross-grain scratches are possible, but can be minimized by stroking the machine back and forth with the grain. The results are excellent on teak, but a final hand sanding of mahogany or other wood that will be varnished pays dividends. Reciprocating power sanders move the paper back and forth to always sand with the grain. The results are similar to hand sanding, which is why these machines are often sold as "finishing sanders."

Circular sanders are generally not recommended for wood finishing. These sanders typically are flat, round rubber disks that install in a ¼-inch drill motor. A set screw holds the sanding disk against the wheel. This type of sander is suitable for removing old paint but not for finish sanding because it creates so many cross-grain scratches.

An exception to the circular sander prohibition is a dual-action sander favored by professional refinishers. Known in the trade as a "D-A," this type of sander is expensive, whether air powered or electric. A D-A is excellent for fairing large contours or sanding flat surfaces.

Dual-action sanders, known as "D-A's," are favorite tools of professional refinishers. The sanding disk simultaneously rotates and orbits, so that swirl marks are all but eliminated. Practice is needed to learn the trick of holding the disk absolutely flat against the surface being sanded. D-A sanders can be used on wood or fiberglass. The rapid spinning of a D-A produces an irritating dust that requires the use of a respirator to protect the lungs. Goggles are also recommended, especially for people who wear contact lenses.

Sanding Paint and Varnish

Old paint or varnish to be top-coated should be cut back aggressively enough to remove the thickness of the new coat. This avoids a thick buildup of paint or varnish. Start the job with 100 grit paper on an electric palm sander. If necessary, drop down to 80 grit—but only under duress. Once the old surface is cut back, move up to 180, and possibly 220, before applying the new coating.

Sanding between fresh coats of paint or varnish requires a much lighter touch and a less aggressive approach. New coats are always soft, so sandpaper cuts quickly. Hand sanding is always safest. On the first one or two coats, work with 220 grit just hard enough to dull the surface and remove any surface dirt imbedded in the coating. Sanding between coats is the best way to get rid of brush marks or other imperfections before the final coat.

Expect soft paint or varnish to clog the abrasive of the sandpaper. The new surface is too soft for sanding if sanding dust turns into rolls or pills beneath the sanding pad. Allow at least twenty-four hours before sanding a new coat of paint or varnish.

Wet Sanding Gel Coat

Hull or deck repairs on fiberglass boats often require sanding the gel coat back to its original smoothness. This is invariably done with wet sandpaper lubricated by water. A rubber sanding block (the kind that holds the sandpaper securely on nails) is recommended, as it will be in and out of the water during the sanding process. Start sanding with 320 or 400 grit paper and work up to at least 1,200 grit. Coarser grits do the fairing work while the finer-grit papers remove sanding scratches and produce the final glass-smooth surface. Wet sanding gel coat takes lots of time and elbow grease. A professional spends hours working up through the grits on a small repair.

Set a bucket of water on a table near the work to avoid a tired back from bending over. A drop of dishwashing detergent in the water acts as a lubricant and reduces the clogging of the sandpaper. Wet out the surface to be sanded with a sponge and dip the sanding block (with paper attached) into the bucket of water. Sand in long, *straight* strokes across the blemish. Never sand in a circle, as the swirl marks will always show in the final result. Rewet the sandpaper whenever it begins to drag, and replace old paper often.

Squeegee the water off from time to time to assess the progress. (Wet gel coat always looks great; defects show only when it is dry.) Use a highlight from a strong, point source light to check fairness. Problems show best in bright light. A rule of thumb is that *when you think you have done all you can do with one grit of paper, you're only half done with that grit.* From 220, move to 320, 600, and finally to 1,200 grit. Final restoration of the original gloss is restored by buffing with a mild fiberglass rubbing compound.

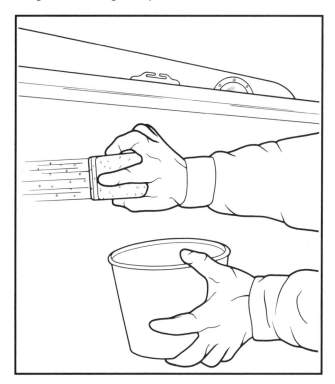

A small bucket of water is necessary when wet sanding fiberglass. The bucket can be hand-held, but it's easier to place it on a small table. Dip the waterproof rubber sanding block and then sand in a straight line, either left-to-right or up-and-down. Sanding in a circle will cause swirl marks. From time to time, check progress by wiping the surface dry with a rubber squeegee.

Burning through the gel coat and into the darker laminate beneath is usually a sign that the gel coat was too thin in that spot and should be built up again. One of the reasons professional gel coat repairs cost so much is the time it takes to properly build up new gel coat and wet sand it to perfect gloss.

PRO TIP

Old clothes and rubber gloves are recommended when wet sanding. A slurry of white sanding dust in water can be expected to drip everywhere. Protect carpets or seat cushions with plastic drop cloths. Wipe up spills or splashes quickly, as dried sanding slurry is hard to remove.

⎈ RUBBING OUT FADED HULLS

Time: One hour per 40 square feet.

Materials: Rubbing compound, applicator, buffing cloths, dust mask.

Tools: Low-speed orbital polisher, safety goggles.

Safety: Power tool safety, eye protection.

Fiberglass gel coat chalks, fades, and eventually stains, no matter how fastidious the owner. Waxing or polishing significantly delays the natural aging process but does not prevent it. Ultraviolet light is responsible for most of the damage. That's why boats in tropical waters tend to chalk and fade faster than those in northern climates. Saltwater is also more harmful than fresh. Weathering breaks down the original smooth surface of the gel coat into millions of microscopic pits. The boat no longer glistens because the micro-pits don't reflect light like the original mirror finish. Dirt in the pits also makes the hull look even older.

Compounding the Hull

Rubbing compound and a good orbital power buffer can restore much of the original shine. "Compounding" a boat physically removes the outer layer of pitted gel coat and exposes a new layer of unweathered an unpitted color underneath. This process also gets rid of minor gel coat scratches. Like sandpaper, rubbing compounds are sold in a variety of grits from coarse to ultrafine.

The grit of a rubbing compound is described as its "cut." Fast-cutting compounds have the coarsest grit. The general rule with fiberglass is to use the mildest rubbing compound that will do the job. If mild compound isn't getting the job done, move to a coarser cut. Never start with coarse cutting compound, as it may do more damage than good.

Professionals often start the initial compounding with a product like Du Pont number 7 red rubbing compound before switching to Du Pont number 101S white compound. Both of these pastes are automotive compounds, which are quicker cutting than those sold for use on fiberglass. Rubbing compounds designed exclusively for fiberglass come in both paste and liquid form. Paste compounds are faster cutting and normally used with a power buffer. Liquids are milder and may be used either with a power buffer or by hand. The typical job starts out with paste compound and finishes with liquid.

CAUTION

Improper use of rubbing compound, especially with a power buffer, can cause expensive damage to gel coat. Too coarse a compound or too much pressure on the buffer will "burn through" the thin layer of gel coat color, exposing the underlying fiberglass laminate. Always start with mild compound and light pressure on a test section. Quit buffing at the first sign of color change, usually a darkening of light colors.

Using a Power Buffer

Work in an area about 4 feet wide and 3 feet deep. Use a disposable bristle brush to apply compound to the surface. A couple of good X-shaped brushstrokes should do. Better to put too little compound on the gel coat than too much. With the buffer turned *off*, use the polishing bonnet to spread the compound over the work area. Don't start the buffer until compound is well distributed over the surface. This avoids spitting compound to the moon when the machine is started.

Start the buffer and move it in large horizontal sweeps across the surface. At first the bonnet will leave a swirl pattern of compound in its wake. In a few minutes, after additional buffing, the compound will begin to disappear and the shiny gel coat will emerge. Heavier pressure on the machine may be required at first, but lighter pressure is needed once the shine begins to show. Complete the entire hull with fast-cutting compound before switching to a milder product for final buffing.

Old, dead compound and microscopic dust from the gel coat build up in the polishing bonnet. This caked buildup prevents the "wool" of the bonnet from properly buffing the surface. Dried compound is removed with a special tool called a "spur" or buffing pad cleaner. These are commonly sold by automotive parts stores. A spur consists of a pistol-grip handle, at the end of which is a rotating wheel with steel fingers that resemble cowboys' spurs. Turn on the buffer and apply the spur to the bonnet. Dust will fly. Most of the "fluff" of the polishing wool of the bonnet will be restored in a few seconds. Spurring is required after every five to seven minutes of actual work.

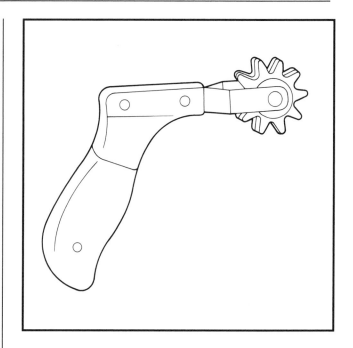

Hardened buffing compound eventually builds up in the polishing bonnet. A special tool known as a "spur" is used to remove it. The rotating star wheel of the spur is held against the spinning bonnet until as much of the old compound as possible is removed.

Final buffing is done with an electrical buffing machine and a special "wool" bonnet. A firm, two-handed grip is necessary in order to put most of the pressure on the center of the tool so that it is spread evenly through the polishing disk. The disk with bonnet must be held flat against the surface. Angling the disk can result in "burning" through the gel coat.

Selecting a Polishing Bonnet

A good polishing bonnet is important to a quality compounding job. Read the instructions on the compound for information on which type of bonnet is best. Here are some general hints:

Wool (or String) Type: This works best with paste compounds intended for rapid cutting. Wool bonnets also work well with waxes and polishes. Although called "wool," most are actually made of cotton or synthetic materials.

Foam Pads: These are intended to work with liquid compounds in the final stages of a compounding job. Use a pad manufactured by the maker of the compound for best results. Foam pads are also excellent for use with many polishes and waxes.

Polishing bonnets should be restricted to one cut of rubbing compound. Never use the same bonnet or pad for both rubbing compound and wax or polish. Check the instructions that come with the bonnet or pad. Many can be tossed into the washing machine and have indefinite lifespans.

VARNISH, THE FINAL TOUCH

> **Time:** One hour per 10 square feet.
>
> **Materials:** Sandpaper, varnish, solvent.
>
> **Tools:** Power sander, scraper, putty knife, sanding block, natural brush, old stocking, rags, tack rags, clean container.
>
> **Safety:** Hand and eye protection from solvent and splashed varnish.

Fiberglass boats use varnished wood only sparingly as trim, but even small amounts give a boat the appearance of being "a proper yacht." Exterior trim needs annual attention to maintain its yacht-like appearance. Interior varnish can usually go for years without refinishing. The work needed to maintain bright wood is more than offset by the admiration of fellow yachtsmen.

Whenever possible, wood trim should be removed from the boat for refinishing. A clean, dust-free shop where the air is still and the temperature doesn't vary by more than 10 degrees is the best place to work. Spills or drips on the shop floor aren't nearly the problem they would be on the interior carpet or upholstery of the boat. Unfortunately, some pieces of wood simply can't be removed for varnishing. Trim strips held in place by screws hidden behind wood bungs are a good example of pieces that have to be refinished in place on the boat.

Old varnish that is tired and dull but otherwise in good condition does not have to be removed. All it needs is a new topcoat or two. Sand off the surface (see "Sanding Wood and Fiberglass" on page 44), tack it down, and lay on a new coat. But if the situation is not so rosy—that is, if the varnish is dry and peeling or has big blisters, or if the wood is turning black under the existing varnish—then there is serious work to be done. In this case, the old varnish must be removed down to bare wood and new protection built up from scratch.

Old varnish that is cracked and peeling must be removed by "wooding down." Old varnish is sometimes so deteriorated that it can be scraped off with a thumbnail. Removal can be done by scraping, sanding, or with chemical strippers.

Wooding Down

The purpose of wooding down is to get back to a smooth wood surface free of old varnish or other contaminants. This allows the building of a totally new protective varnish coating. Wooding down requires considerable effort, and thus should be reserved only for cases where the old varnish is beyond repair.

Old varnish can be removed by sanding, scraping, or with a chemical paint stripper. Sanding is time-consuming but has the distinct advantage of safety. There's far less possibility of damaging the wood by sanding than there is by scraping. Also, sanding does not require strong chemicals that can damage gel coat or cause chemical burns to the skin. If paint remover is necessary, be sure to get one formulated for fiberglass. Ordinary paint removers can soften fiberglass gel coat and should not be used on wood that is still mounted on the boat.

Surface Preparation

About 90 percent of the job of varnishing is surface preparation. Varnish wants to go over as smooth a surface as possible, so work up through the grits with sandpaper. Vacuum the wood thoroughly to remove as much sanding dust as possible. Then use finger tips to find rough spots that the eye can't see. Remove these with fine sandpaper and vacuum again.

PRO TIP

Always use plain white paper towels when decontaminating surfaces with solvents. Cloth rags are usually contaminated with the silicone-based fabric softeners found in most laundry detergents. This is especially true of household rags made out of old bedsheets or clothing. Solvents such as mineral spirits will transfer the fabric softeners onto the surface being wiped clean. The result is more contamination, not less. Plain white paper towels contain no potential contaminants. Avoid towels with printed designs, as printing inks may cause contamination.

Chemical contamination of the wood will prevent adhesion of the varnish. Even the natural oil from human hands can be a problem. Get rid of contaminants by wiping the wood with mineral spirits on a paper towel. Let the wood dry overnight before proceeding.

Making varnish stick to teak is problematical at best, because of its natural oils. A wipe-down with acetone on a white paper towel will remove most of the natural oils from the surface of the wood. Turn the paper towel often and work in a well-ventilated area away from open flames. Wear hand and eye protection.

Staining

Wood is stained for cosmetic reasons. Restoration of a classic boat requires stains that exactly match those used by the original manufacturer. That's why stains bearing the names Chris-Craft, Lyman, and Egg Harbor can still be found even though none of those companies build wooden boats any longer. On a modern boat, the reason for staining wood is most often to blend a number of pieces into a pleasing whole. Planks cut from different trees are never exactly the same color. Staining reduces or eliminates these natural color differences.

Marine stains are usually "filler stains" that come as thick pastes. *Do not apply filler stain straight from the can!* Mix the paste with turpentine or paint thinner to obtain a working consistency similar to that of thin oil paint. Brush stain onto the wood *across the grain* and then allow to dry partially. It will slowly lose its glossy appearance and begin to turn "flat."

Immediately after it flats, start wiping across the grain (yes, *across* the grain) to push as much of this paste as possible into the grain. Wiping *with* the grain would remove the paste from the grain. Turn the rag often and discard rags that become filled with paste to prevent streaks. Paste stain becomes rock hard if not wiped off at the proper time. Sometimes, a bad situation can be turned around by dampening the wiping rag with paint thinner.

Final rubbing is done with a dry rag, buffing *with* the grain to remove horizontal streaks. Buff lightly so as to not remove the filler from the grain. All this work of using a paste filler stain should result in filling the grain of the wood to provide the necessary smooth surface for the varnish.

Oil-based stains can be used beneath all conventional and polyurethane varnishes. *Never use oil-based stain beneath clear epoxy base coats,* such as WEST System's. Epoxies do not properly bond to oil-based stains. Aniline wood stains are safe under epoxies. These stains come in a powder form that can be mixed with either water or alcohol. Mixing aniline powder in water produces a slower-drying stain but one that is more controllable. An alcohol mix dries too quickly for staining by hand with a rag.

The Base Coat

The first coat of varnish seals the surface and soaks into the wood, providing a good base for future coats. At this stage, penetration into the wood is far more important than gloss or good buildup. That's why all varnish manufacturers recommend thinning first coats by as much as 50 percent. Thinned varnish soaks into the wood better than thick varnish straight from the can.

Thinning marine varnish is the expensive way to get a good sealer coat. Much less expensive and equally effective is a coat of Pettit's 2018 Clear Sealer. This type of product is really a thin varnish without ultraviolet inhibitors and other ingredients necessary for a long-lasting final coat. It penetrates deeply into the wood and dries within four hours. Because it dries quickly, a base coat and a first finish coat can be applied in one day.

Teak requires special sealer designed to suppress the wood's natural oil. Pettit's rubber-based 2012 Super Dry Sealer is formulated for this job.

Epoxy Resin Base Coat

Clear epoxy makes an excellent base coat under conventional or two-part polyurethane varnishes. Be sure to use an epoxy resin and hardener specifically blended for clear coating. Bonding resins have a tendency to turn cloudy over time, obscuring the grain and color of the wood. Coating resins do not become cloudy. WEST System recommends using its 105 Epoxy Resin with its 207 Special Coating Hardener for maximum clarity.

Roll the epoxy onto the wood using a foam roller cover. Tip out any bubbles with a foam brush. Additional epoxy coats can be applied as soon as the one on the deck has cured to a rubber-like stage. At least three thin epoxy coats are recommended. Let the final coat cure at least twenty-four hours before sanding and top-coating with varnish.

Cured epoxy base coats often develop a waxy substance on their surface known as "amine blush." This is produced in the curing process and is not harmful except that it will prevent the adhesion of varnish or other top coats. Amine blush can be removed by scrubbing the surface with a plastic sponge and clear water. Let the epoxy dry thoroughly before sanding or top-coating. Epoxies are subject to rapid deterioration by ultraviolet light. They must be top-coated with a varnish containing ultraviolet inhibitors.

Top Coats

Whether conventional or epoxy, the sealer coat must be prepared before the final top coats are applied. Sand conventional varnish sealer coats lightly with 220 grit paper, touching only the flat surfaces, because the coating on outside corners is thin and easy to burn through. Epoxy base coats are more rugged and can be sanded with 180 grit.

After sanding, use two commercial tack rags to remove dust from the surface. The first gets 99 percent of the dust, but the important wipedown is the second rag, which gets the remaining 1 percent. The tack rags available from paint and hardware stores are cheesecloth saturated with a sticky substance that picks up dust or dirt. Turn the cloth often to expose new stickum.

Marine varnish should never be used straight from the can. Always pour a working amount into a clean container and immediately reseal the original container. This keeps the stock varnish in the can from getting dirt or dust in it. Pour varnish slowly to prevent the formation of bubbles. Filter it through a piece of women's panty hose to remove unwanted crud if a disposable paper filter funnel is not available. Old-timers always pour their varnish into a glass container because tin cans may contain food residue that can contaminate the varnish.

Two thin coats of varnish are better than a thick one, because thick coats tend to sag or form "lace curtains" on vertical surfaces. Paradoxical as it sounds, sags and runs are usually signals that the varnish is too thick and needs thinning. Sags occur when the surface of the new coat begins to dry while the underlying varnish remains liquid and continues to flow. A thinner coat dries more evenly, as there is no underlying liquid to run downhill.

Don't use generic paint thinner or mineral spirits to thin marine coatings. Always choose the proprietary thinner specified by the varnish manufacturer; it will contain special additives to prevent runs or sags and make brushing easier. Mix thinner into stock varnish with a smooth, easy motion that does not raise bubbles. Being squeaky-clean and avoiding bubbles are two ways to prevent dust and pockmarks in the final finish.

Varnish Application

Dip the brush gently into the varnish and pat it out on the side of the container. Don't wipe the brush on the side of the container, *pat it*. Wiping out the excess on the container rim creates rafts of air bubbles on top of the varnish in the can. Those bubbles can ruin the final finish.

Apply varnish with light pressure. Don't "scrub" the varnish onto the surface or you'll create bubbles. Refill the brush whenever it begins to drag, but avoid building too thick a coat.

"Tipping out" is the final touch to applying varnish. Use light pressure with just the tips of the brush to smooth out imperfections in the wet var-

Varnish should always be poured from its original factory can into a clean container for application. Straining the stock varnish removes any dust or other contaminants. This paper funnel is commercially available, but several thicknesses of women's stockings work just as well. Pour only enough for the job at hand, and never return used varnish to the stock container.

nish. Begin the tipping stroke before making contact with the surface; in this way, you will avoid brush marks caused by starting the stroke on the wet surface. Ending a stroke on wet varnish will not leave a brush mark; just lift the brush quickly from the surface while it's still in motion.

Minor brush marks in the wet film are quite normal and acceptable. They should level themselves as the varnish dries. If brush marks do not level out, try thinning the varnish slightly for the next coat. Work with deliberate haste. There is little time to "tip out" the varnish, perhaps three to five minutes, before it begins to form a skin. Any touch of the brush to that skin is sure to cause conditions called "orange peel" or "alligatoring" on the surface of the wet varnish.

Have an assistant continuously walk around the job checking for skips or dry areas. The person varnishing is never able to see them as well as an observer who is constantly moving from one vantage point to another.

Never go back to fix problem areas in wet varnish once it has been tipped out. Any repair attempts will be worse than the initial problem. A skip or dry spot can only be corrected by letting the varnish dry, sanding the surface and applying another coat. There's no other way. Attempts to fix problems always result in worse damage that requires heavier sanding. Many times, the sanding necessary to remove "orange peel" exposes bare wood. Suddenly, a simple fix becomes a major repair.

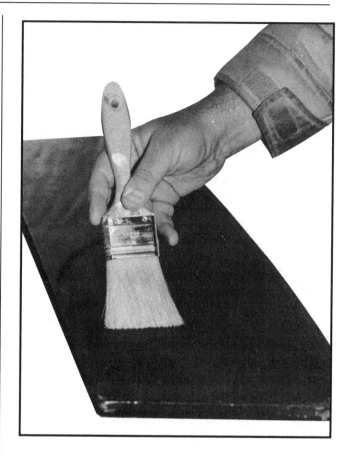

A comfortable grip on the brush is necessary when applying varnish. The bristles should press lightly against the wood and the motion should be a smooth, even stroke. Use small sticks to hold the board off the work table; this will allow you to coat the edges along with the top.

Sanding Between Coats

Sanding between coats removes the gloss and provides a better surface (or "tooth") for the next coat. It also smoothes out imperfections, such as brushstrokes, dirt, and insects entombed in the wet varnish. Light pressure with 220 or 280 grit sandpaper is usually sufficient for sanding between coats. Avoid power sanders, as they cut too quickly. A hand sanding block doesn't get out of control so easily. Stay away from sanding sharp edges as this is almost certain to break through the finish.

The surface should get smoother with every ad-

regard to the next coat of varnish. Wet sanded varnish must be wiped dry and then allowed to air dry for an additional twenty-four hours to insure that all traces of water have evaporated.

Working Conditions

Varnish works best at the same temperature and humidity conditions at which the human body is most comfortable. This may not be the most scientific way of assessing weather conditions, but it works well enough for the purposes at hand. Avoid working in direct sunlight, especially when varnishing a vertical surface. Sunlight causes the varnish to skin off too quickly, so that it can't be tipped out properly. The sun also warms the wet varnish, making it almost impossible to prevent sags and runs. If work must be done in direct sunlight, use the boat's winter tarp as a temporary sun shield.

Varnish Brushes

Professionals insist on high-quality, pure badger bristle brushes set in metal ferrules. A good badger brush will cost fifty bucks anywhere it can be found—and not many stores carry brushes of this quality. Any affordable high-quality natural bristle brush (China bristle, for example) is an acceptable alternative.

Pick a brush with long bristles for good flexibility. The ends of the bristles should be split ("flagged") to hold the varnish and spread it smoothly. Expect to spend up to fifteen dollars for a 2-inch bristle brush. Never—*never*—buy a brush with bristles made of nylon or other man-made materials. Varnish flows too quickly out of nylon bristles.

Do not clean varnish brushes between coats. Instead, suspend them in mineral spirits so that the solvent completely covers the bristles. Suspend-

"Tipping out" wet varnish requires a different grip from that used during the initial application. Pressure on the bristles is very light and the stroke is always made with the grain. Always start tipping strokes off of the work. Bring the brush onto the work at an edge. Strokes can be terminated in the middle of the work by lifting the brush with a slight twisting motion.

ditional new coat of varnish. By the third or fourth coat the grain should be completely filled. Some fastidious refinishers wet sand between the final two coats with 600 or 800 grit paper for ultimate smoothness. There is, however, one possible pitfall to wet sanding: Water used in this process is, technically speaking, a chemical contaminant with

ing brushes is easy if a ³⁄₁₆-inch hole is drilled in the handle just above the ferrule. Cut a piece of coat hanger long enough to span the top of the container. Slip the wire through the holes in the brush handles and suspend the wire over the solvent. To go back to work, simply shake excess mineral spirits out of the brushes and resume varnishing.

When the job is done, clean varnish brushes at least three times in fresh paint thinner or mineral spirits. Work the thinner well into the heel of the brush near the metal ferrule. The thinner used for the final cleaning should be almost as clear after use as when it came from the can. Shake any remaining thinner out of the bristles before washing the brush with gentle soap and lukewarm water. Rinse thoroughly, then form the brush into its original shape and hang it to dry in its original paper wrapper to make sure the bristles hold their shape as they dry.

Multiple Coats

Multiple coats are the secret to a long-lasting varnish job. Above the Mason-Dixon line, boats need a minimum of six coats on exterior wood. Apply two more coats for every five degrees of latitude closer to the equator to fight ultraviolet light, which destroys varnish. Less exposure to ultraviolet allows boats up north to get up to a full season out of a varnish job while boats in southern climes usually need refresher coats once or twice during the summer. In the ultraviolet-rich Caribbean even a dozen coats may have a lifespan measured in weeks. Exposure to salt water also reduces the lifespan of varnish.

⚙

HOOKING UP 12-VOLT WIRING

Time: n/a

Materials: Wire per specifications.

Tools: Diagonal cutters, crimping tool.

Safety: n/a

Primary electric power on most U.S.-built pleasure boats is nominally 12 volts, direct current. This is in conformity with the automotive industry, on which boating depends for inboard gasoline engines. The benefit of this is that a boat's 12-volt system offers relatively little hazard of electrocution. The drawback is that low-voltage systems are subject to substantial current losses in long wires. Voltage loss is particularly critical when installing VHF marine radios. A small drop in voltage can translate into a substantial drop in transmitting range.

For instance, a 1-volt drop is virtually inconsequential in household 115-volt alternating-current systems. It amounts to less than a 1-percent loss in power. But in a boat's 12-volt system, the same 1-volt drop represents a whopping 8-percent loss. A power loss of this magnitude can seriously interfere with a loran-C receiver or reduce the output and transmiting range of a VHF radio transmitter.

Nominal Versus Actual Voltage

Although we say that boats have "12-volt DC" electrical systems, in actuality they operate on two voltages. The lead-acid storage battery that starts the engine actually puts out 12 volts when fully charged. This is the voltage on the electrical system when the engine is not running. However, once the engine starts, the alternator delivers 13.4 volts to the system. This higher voltage is necessary to maintain the charge in the battery. Be sure to remember this 1.4 volt increase when measuring boat voltages or choosing light bulbs.

Wire Gauge

Wire sizes are measured by the American Wire Gauge (AWG) system. Under this system, each size wire is specified by a number, or "gauge." Large-diameter wires have small numbers while small-diameter wires have large numbers. Thus, an 18-gauge wire is smaller than a 12-gauge. Battery cables are usually the largest wires on the boat, typically 6 or 4 gauge.

The following two tables indicate the size wire to be chosen in critical and noncritical applications. A *critical* application is one where even a minor voltage drop may produce an unacceptable result.

CRITICAL APPLICATIONS
Wiring Size for 3-Percent Voltage Drop

Amps on Circuit	Length of Wire (in feet)				
	10	15	20	25	30
5	18 gauge	16	14	12	12
10	14	12	10	10	10
15	12	10	10	8	8
20	10	10	8	6	6
25	10	8	6	6	6

Table 2.6

NONCRITICAL APPLICATIONS
Wiring Size for 10-Percent Voltage Drop

Amps on Circuit	Length of Wire (in feet)				
	10	15	20	25	30
5	18 gauge	18	18	18	18
10	18	18	16	16	14
15	18	16	14	14	12
20	16	14	14	12	12
25	16	14	12	12	10

Table 2.7

Electronic equipment and navigation lights are two critical applications.

Ordinary interior lighting, such as a reading lamp over a bunk, would be considered *noncritical*. Keep in mind that although it is never a mistake to use a wire that is too large, it's always wrong to use one that's too small.

Solid wire is never acceptable in boats. Vibrations from the engine and the passage of the hull through the waves cause solid wire to fatigue and break. Flexible stranded wire is approved for marine application because it is far less susceptible to vibration fatigue. If possible, choose wire in which each strand has been individually tinned, as tinning makes the wire less subject to corrosion.

Insulation Color Coding

It's the nature of boats for the electrical system to become a rat's nest of brightly colored wires. Individual conductors are wrapped into bundles or stuffed into conduits between the engine compartment and control console. Even with a schematic diagram, tracing an individual circuit can be a nightmare. That's why most boat builders follow an industry code of standard wiring colors in which each circuit has an identifying color of insulation on the wires. No law forces the use of this color code, so expect minor variations from brand to brand as well as from boat to boat within the production of one builder.

Wires can be identified either by the color of their plastic insulation or by colored sleeves on the ends, where the wires attach to switches, fuses, and accessories. Some builders may also identify wires by numbered tags that are keyed to a wiring diagram. When installing accessories it is always best to continue the standard marine color code (see Table 2.8).

Connections, Splices, and Terminals

Boat wiring lives in a damp, corrosive atmosphere. Even the best electrical equipment deteriorates as the result of exposure to saltwater spray. Salt in the air finds its way onto exposed contacts or into splices and connections. As such, these crystals do little harm. But, each grain of salt attracts water vapor from the air and the combination of water and salt really gets corrosion going! That's why it pays to use only marine-grade electrical materials.

Crimp-on connectors and splices have become universal in the boating industry. Factories like them because they install quickly, so one worker can do a lot of wiring in a day's time. Backyard workers appreciate crimp-on connectors for the same reason: they're fast and easy. All that's needed to make strong connections is the crimping tool and the proper fittings. The crimping tool also doubles as a wire cutter and skinner. Kits containing a good tool and a selection of eye, spade, and butt connectors are available.

All crimp-on connectors are sized according to the gauge of the wire being used. Using too small a connector will not allow all of the individual strands of the wire to be captured. This seriously reduces the current-carrying capacity of the circuit. On the other hand, using too large a connector results in a loose joint that is almost certain to fall apart on the first dark night when electric light is needed.

The wire is skinned back using the crimping tool. The amount of conductor to be exposed depends on the gauge and the brand of connector. Use the wire-skinner opening marked for the gauge of wire to avoid cutting individual strands. Insert the bare wire into the connector and then place the connector in the jaws of the crimping tool. The tool has several different openings for different size connectors. Crimp down hard! One crimp is enough for small-gauge connectors. Two or more

BOAT WIRING COLOR CODE

Wire Color	Circuit Description	Typical Uses of Circuit
Black	Negative Mains	Return wire to battery
Dark Gray	Navigation Lights	From fuse or switch to lights
Purple	Ignition	Switch to coil and instruments
Purple	Instruments	Distribution panel to instruments
Dark Blue	Lights	Distribution panel to lights
Green	Bonding	Non-current boat bonding system
Brown	Generator	Armature to regulator
Brown	Pumps	Fuse or switch to pumps
Tan	Water Temp	Temperature sender to gauge
Yellow	Alternator	Field to regulator field
Yellow	Bilge Blower	Fuse or switch to blower motors
Yellow with Red Stripe	Starter	Switch to solenoid
Orange	Accessories	Ammeter to alternator and accessory fuses to switches
Red	Positive Mains	Main power, particularly unfused from the battery
Pink	Fuel Gauge	Fuel tank sender to gauge
White	Negative Mains	Return wire to battery

Table 2.8

A crimping tool can be used to skin the wire before attaching a connector. Place the wire in the skinning jaws, making sure to use the opening of the correct gauge. Pull off the insulation with a smooth jerk.

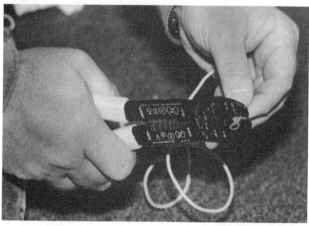

Insert the skinned wire into the connector and then use the tool to crimp the connector tightly onto the wire. Use the crimping jaws specified for the size of the connector. Some tools are marked with a color code that matches the plastic insulation on the connector.

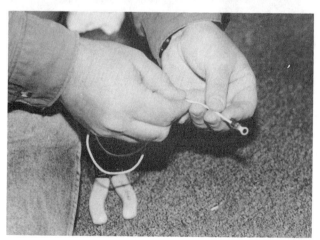

Inspect finished connections. This 18-gauge eye connector needed only one crimp. Larger-gauge connectors may require two or more crimps.

crimps are necessary on larger fittings. The result should be a mechanically and electrically sound connection.

Eyes and captive spade lugs are used on the ends of boat wiring for connection to distribution panels. Neither will disconnect if the connecting screw loosens from vibration. Spade ("push-on") connectors are seldom used except on some switches and other small parts not large enough for screw terminals.

Splicing wires is never recommended if it is possible to use one continuous length of wire. Even the best splice invites the possibility of corrosion, especially if that splice is hidden in the joiner work.

A variety of approaches exists to fighting corrosion within crimp connectors. One school believes in spraying terminals and connectors every season with a moisture-displacing lubricant such as WD-40. Other people prefer the messy solution of pushing silicone sealant into the ends of the connectors where the wires emerge. Another approach is to seal the connector with heat-shrinkable tubing. Still others crimp their connectors and then solder them with resin-core radio solder.

CHAPTER 3

THE HULL

The hull *is* the boat.

Hand-rubbed teak or oiled walnut in the saloon may impress the guests, but it's the hull that keeps everything afloat. That's why hull maintenance takes top priority when fitting out, the only practical time to examine or repair underwater gear. Nearly all the jobs in this chapter require the boat to be hauled and firmly blocked in its cradle on shore.

Crew safety requires that the blocking be checked prior to the start of every work session, particularly in spring. Winter frost heaves and spring rains soften the earth supporting the cradle, creating a potentially dangerous situation. Boats blocked only on jack stands are particularly suspect.

Hard-shelled marine animals—barnacles— were once only a saltwater problem. Those lucky enough to sail the Great Lakes and other large bodies of fresh water felt smugly superior because they didn't have to fight pesky barnacles. Well, times have changed and now the zebra mussel is becoming the freshwater barnacle. Everyone, in salt water or fresh, now has a problem with hard-shell marine growth that robs both power and speed. Other than never launching the boat, the preventative for barnacle or zebra mussel growth is an application of a good antifouling bottom paint.

The newest antifouling coatings work by making the hull too slippery for marine growth to attach itself. The older technology of traditional bottom paints works by poisoning any barnacles, zebra mussels, or slime that has homesteaded on the boat. Because of environmental laws, the only poison ("biocide") currently legal for use on pleasure boats is copper. Freshly applied bottom paint is full of copper, but during the season this biocide leaches out of the paint.

After six to twelve months (depending on lati-

APPLYING ANTIFOULING PAINT

Time: For a 25-foot boat: one weekend to sand, four hours to paint. Time goes up geometrically with size of the boat.

Materials: Sandpaper, dust masks, painter's sock, disposable gloves, fiberglass dewaxer, paint thinner, masking tape, disposable bristle brushes, aluminum foil, black-foam 9-inch roller covers, 2-inch disposable rollers, rags.

Tools: Electric sander, goggles, stiff-blade putty knife, paint roller tray, 9-inch paint roller frame, long handle for roller.

Safety: Protection for eyes, lungs, and skin from potentially toxic sanding dust. Electric tool safety, particularly when working on wet ground. Be sure boat is blocked properly before working underneath.

tude, water salinity, and other factors), so much biocide has leached out that the paint no longer repels growth. A leached-out antifouling paint may still display bright color and be well adhered to the hull. There is no way to tell by eye if last year's antifouling paint is still active. This is why traditional bottom paints must be applied fresh every season (or more often in tropical waters).

Co-polymer antifouling paints were introduced about a decade ago with claims of "multi-year success." These claims were true for the first co-polymer paints, which contained tin as the biocide. The banning of tin put the whole question of multi-year paints in limbo. New co-polymer paints with copper biocide appear to last more than one season in northern waters. However, there are those who question the ecological safety of copper and copper compounds in the marine environment. This issue is likely to become a future battleground between boat owners and the "green revolution."

ALUMINUM BOAT WARNING

Never apply copper-based antifouling paint to an aluminum boat or to aluminum lower units of outboard motors or outdrives. Copper and aluminum exposed to salt water will cause galvanic corrosion of the aluminum. Tin-based antifouling paints must be used on aluminum boats, but these must be applied by a licensed applicator. Depending upon state laws, small spray cans of tin-based antifouling paint may be available for outdrive lower units. Another alternative is to use one of the non-metallic antifouling coatings now coming onto the market.

Preparation of New Bottoms

Fiberglass boats come from the factory with an invisible wax coating. This invisible coating is the remanent of release wax that allowed the hull to be "popped out" of the female mold in which it was built. Mold release wax also happens to be a pretty fair paint release agent. If it is not removed, bottom paint will not adhere. The lazy man's way to remove the mold release agent is to put a new boat into the water for a season without bottom paint. In addition to getting rid of the release wax, this procedure also grows an exceptional crop of weeds, barnacles, or zebra muscles.

Professionals prepping a factory-new boat normally reach for a can of fiberglass dewaxer. This liquid cleaning agent closely resembles mineral spirits and requires similar safety precautions. Follow the instructions exactly, particularly the part about using clean rags and turning them often. Dewaxing agent can also be purchased from most paint stores that serve professionals. In a pinch, mineral spirits can be used.

Sanding a new boat's bottom is not absolutely necessary, although many experts recommend a dry sanding with 220 grit paper to give a "tooth" to the gel coat. Tooth is thought to improve paint adhesion. Sand only *after* the bottom has been dewaxed. Sanding prior to dewaxing just forces the mold release agent deep into the gel coat where it becomes almost impossible to remove.

Prepping Existing Paint

Old paint on the bottom should have been power-washed at the end of the previous season to remove all marine growth. Dried grass or slime may seem solid enough when the boat's in the cradle, but it will turn soft after launching. Anyone foolish enough to paint over last year's mung is sure to experience paint adhesion failure. The new paint will simply peel off the old biological fouling.

There is no absolute need to sand the bottom if the old paint is clean, smooth, and well adhered to the hull. New paint of exactly the same brand and type can be applied directly over clean old paint. However, the entire bottom is seldom smooth enough or well enough adhered for new paint without some prep work. When in doubt, sand and scrape. Virtually all bottom paint failures are caused by improper or incomplete surface preparation.

Using mechanical sanders to remove old bottom paint is dusty, dirty work. Skin, eye, and breathing protection is always required. Care must be exercised when using electric tools on wet ground or when working outdoors.

Sanding—when it means lying flat beneath the boat while working overhead—is tiring and unrewarding work. Within minutes arms ache almost to tears as dust and flakes of old paint float into eyes and nose. Ah, the rewards of pleasure boating! There is nothing that can be done to take away the unpleasantness of sanding the bottom.

There's still plenty of biocide in that old paint dust. Anything that is toxic to barnacles can't be too good for human beings. Be sure to wear protective clothing. A dust mask will prevent you from inhaling potentially toxic dust, while a watch cap will keep your hair clean. Goggles will keep paint dust and chips out of your eyes.

Masking the Waterline

After sanding, the final preparation step is masking off the waterline. Use masking tape at least 1-inch wide in case of an "oops" over the line. Buy good tape. Cheap masking tape gives a fuzzy line caused by wet paint wicking underneath. For absolute best results, try 3M's Fine Line tape. If this isn't available, look for the type of clear plastic strapping tape that is reinforced with nylon threads. Strapping tape also cuts a sharp line and won't break when pulled away from the hull.

No matter what type of tape is used, do not leave it on the hull any longer than necessary. Paper tape *must* be removed before the paint dries or it will be virtually impossible to get it off. Wear disposable gloves to protect against wet paint. Pull the tape straight away from the hull and ball it between the hands. Avoid letting wet tape contact the hull topsides.

Application

Antifouling paint must be thoroughly mixed to disperse the biocide. Best mixing is done in a paint store by a mechanical paint shaker. Never thin bottom paint in order to "stretch" it to cover more area. Antifouling should be applied just as it comes from the can. Thinning to increase coverage reduces the amount of biocide applied, which just reduces protection against marine growth. Some unusual working conditions may require thinning for workability, but read and follow the instructions and always use the correct thinner.

Bottom paint should never be sprayed by an amateur. The stuff is just too toxic for personal safety without professional respirators and other protective gear. Instead, apply it with a roller and brush. The job will go as quickly as spraying, but with far less health risk.

Start by "cutting in" around the masking tape with a brush. Use a pure bristle disposable brush to apply a stripe about three inches wide all around the boat. Disposable foam brushes may dissolve in antifouling coatings. Paint in X-shapes rather than straight strokes to avoid horizontal streaks around the waterline. Be sure to wear rubber gloves to keep paint off of hands. Not only is bottom paint potentially toxic, but it also stains skin more than other types of paint.

Choose medium-nap foam roller covers for the rest of the job. Thick-nap covers will give too rough a texture, while thin nap rollers apply too thin of a coat. Buy several roller covers, as the solvents in antifouling paint tend to dissolve their cardboard cores. The best covers are found in professional paint stores. Tell the salesman they will be used in bottom paint. He'll select covers least likely to dissolve. And ask for a couple of the disposable 2-inch rollers that professionals use for quick trim jobs. These mini-rollers will do tight spots that can't be reached with a full-size 9-inch roller.

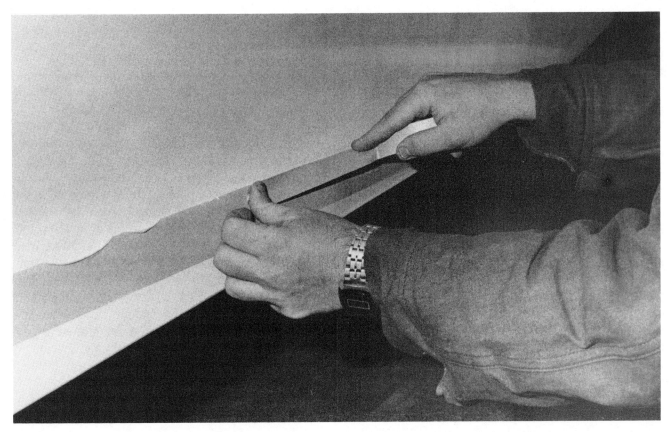

Mask off the waterline either with 3-M's special Fine Line tape or with regular masking tape. Right handers should use their left hand to anchor tape while controlling the roll in their right. Allow the adhesive to "bite" on its own before rubbing down the tape with the left hand. Move backwards around the hull, taping 4-to-5-foot stretches at a time.

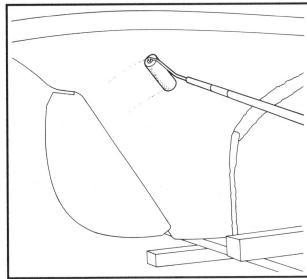

The easiest way to apply antifouling bottom paint is with a long-handled roller. This allows the painter to stand comfortably beside the hull while rolling the far reaches of the keel. Most roller frames have threaded handles that match standard mop handles.

Apply antifouling paint generously, rolling out only lap marks and areas obviously drowning in paint. A major mistake is trying to "push" the paint too far with the roller. Remember, overly thin coats won't give the desired protection. Most roller frames have an opening in the handle that is threaded to accept either a mop handle or a regular extension handle. Using an extension allows painting the bottom without actually getting under the boat.

Cleanup

Avoid plastic roller-pan inserts intended to aid in cleanup. Solvents in antifouling paint can dissolve some plastics. Instead, line the roller pan with aluminum foil from the kitchen. When the job's done, dispose of the foil and the pan is clean. Cut the foil somewhat larger than the pan so that it can be used to wrap dirty roller covers and brushes for disposal.

Environmental Considerations

Bottom paint is toxic. All soiled brushes, roller covers, and pan liners should be disposed of properly. Disposal methods vary in different regions of the country. Check with the boatyard operator for the proper way to get rid of antifouling paint trash. This applies at home too. Don't just throw the old can and rags in the trash. Get rid of it properly.

It may not be long before individual owners won't be allowed to sand the bottoms of their boats. Regulations now on the books are forcing boatyards to capture the toxic sanding dust and dispose of it in approved methods. There is no way that this can be done if each owner sands the bottom of his boat in the time-honored way out in the boatyard. Capturing the dust can only be done in special pits and by using special sanding equipment. Look for the day when we'll all have to pay to have this job done—and pay dearly.

FIXING OSMOTIC BLISTERS

Time: Ninety minutes per blister (spread over time).

Materials: Sanding disks, sandpaper, epoxy resin, thickening agent, acetone, mixing bucket, rags, disposable gloves, disposable brushes.

Tools: Disk sander, putty knife, sanding block, goggles.

Safety: Goggles for eye protection when sanding; goggles and gloves for protection against epoxy and acetone. Be sure boat is properly blocked on cradle.

From the outset, let's make it clear that we're talking about osmotic blistering in fiberglass laminates below the waterline. These are not simple construction faults involving an air bubble trapped between the gel coat and underlying layers of glass and resin. Rather, osmotic blisters are chemical in origin and develop only after the boat is launched and water begins to permeate into the fabric of the hull. Unlike air bubbles, osmotic blisters usually contain a foul-smelling liquid when broken open.

The Blister Controversy

Bottom blisters are the most controversial problem in boat repair. Everyone has a private theory or two on why one boat gets the pox on its bottom while other boats in the same harbor do not. Scientific research shows that blisters originate both in the compounding of the resins and in the layup of the hull at the boat factory. Potential blister sites lay dormant until the boat is launched and water osmosis begins, initiating a chemical process that results in boat pox. Some boats get a full-blown case with blisters fore and aft on both sides of the keel. Others get only an isolated blister or two, while a few lucky hulls go through life blister-free.

Epoxy Works Best

The consensus of boatyards is that blister repairs are best done with epoxy materials. Without a doubt, the people at Gougeon Brothers have considerable experience working with marine epoxy resins. Before attempting any repairs with epoxy materials, send for their booklets "Gelcoat Blisters Diagnosis, Repair, and Prevention" and "Fiberglass Boat Repair and Maintenance with WEST System Epoxy." There is a three-dollar charge for these booklets. Write: Gougeon Brothers, Inc., P.O. Box X908, Bay City, Michigan 48707; telephone: (517)684-7286.

Serious Osmotic Blistering

Osmotic blistering can range from a few small blisters to a bottom pocked with what appears to be terminal acne. Boats that tend toward the latter situation need professional care. Ask a qualified marine surveyor to determine the extent of the problem. With that information, contact boat repair facilities with the best reputation for quality work. Don't shop price. Shop quality. The future health of the boat depends on the quality of the blister repair work.

Repairing a major case of osmotic blisters is beyond the capability of the amateur. Equipment to do the work correctly is far too expensive for a one-time job. Current philosophy calls for "peeling" the old gel coat off of the bottom to expose the underlying fiberglass. A precision machine is needed to remove an exact thickness of material. Depth of the cut is predetermined by the operator. In most cases, only the gel coat is removed so that the underlying laminate of fiberglass cloth and resin remains intact. This preserves the structural integrity of the hull.

Severe blistering may require the removal of one or more layers of fiberglass laminate. This is serious surgery that reduces the original strength of the hull. All fiberglass cloth removed must be replaced, a tricky job since the new cloth or mat is applied *overhead* to the bottom of the boat. Technicians working beneath the hull have to force drippy resin and floppy glass cloth to adhere against the force of gravity. This is definitely *not* a job for amateurs!

Drying Time Is Critical

The peeled hull must be allowed to dry thoroughly so that water trapped in the laminate evaporates. This takes a long time for some boats. Some people suggest storing the peeled boat indoors over a winter layup and completing repairs in the spring. The interior bilge must be absolutely dry during storage. All water must be sponged out of sumps and low spots inside the hull. If bilge water is not removed, it will continue to permeate the laminate and retard or prevent drying. Drying can be speeded up by the application of heat under controlled conditions. Really advanced shops may resort to exotic vacuum drying techniques.

There is no way to tell by eye or by feel if a hull is dry enough to accept the barrier coat. Regular moisture readings taken with a professional moisture meter are needed. Readings should be taken at many places around the hull and averaged together. Over time, readings should show a steady decline in the moisture content of the laminate until it stabilizes.

If a moisture meter is not available, WEST System recommends taping 6-inch squares of plastic kitchen wrap to the hull at several locations using vinyl electrician's tape. Moisture in the laminate should condense inside these plastic patches. Lift each patch at regular intervals and wipe out any condensation. The hull is dry enough to take barrier coat when little or no condensation has been detected under the patches in several weeks.

Finish the Job Yourself

Once the bottom is peeled and dried, the owner may step back into the picture to do some or all of the remaining work. A variety of paint and chemical companies make repair compounds and barrier coatings designed to prevent future blistering.

All of them are based on the concept of providing a waterproof barrier between the fiberglass and the surrounding water. Since the bottom never gets wet, osmosis can't take place and new blisters should not occur.

Blister craters should be filled with an epoxy putty before applying the barrier coat. Marine-Tex by Travco Labs is a favorite product for this purpose. Pettit's 7020/7025 Epoxy Fairing Compound is a similar product. WEST System recommends mixing either its 407 or its 410 low-density filler with a standard resin mixture to make a working putty. The advantage of mixing

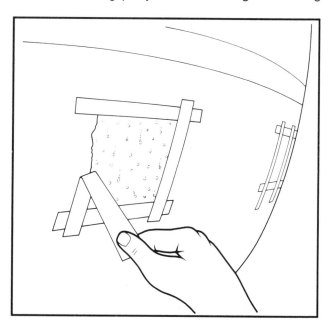

WEST System suggests using ordinary plastic kitchen wrap to test a peeled hull for moisture. Tape small squares of wrap to the hull using black electrician's tape. Be sure to seal the edges of the wrap so that air cannot enter. Moisture contained in the fiberglass laminate will condense inside the patches. From time to time, open the patches and wipe out this condensation. When little or no water condenses in the majority of patches, the hull is dry enough for application of an epoxy barrier coat.

putty on the spot is that the thickness can be varied to fit the situation.

Epoxy putty should be troweled into blister cavities and allowed to "kick." WEST System recommends precoating the area inside all blister cavities with unthickened epoxy resin before applying the putty. This two-step process insures the best possible bond with the fiberglass laminate. Unusually deep craters may require a second application. Hardened putty should be sanded smooth and fair with the surrounding areas of the hull.

The next step is covering the entire bottom below the waterline with a barrier coat (or coats). The Interlux InterProtect system is an example of a two-step process that requires two coats of 1000 Base Coat and four or five coats of InterProtect 2000. Barrier coats are somewhat tricky to apply since the materials are neither paints nor putties. The instructions accompanying the barrier product *must* be followed exactly, especially regarding times between application of successive coats.

The WEST System recommends at least six coats of its 105 resin mixed with the correct proportion of 205 hardener. The first coat should be just clear epoxy. Subsequent coats should be mixed with 422 barrier coat additive to improve moisture resistance. All coats should be applied in one day to avoid the necessity of removing the amine blush and sanding. Additional coats of epoxy may be applied as soon as the current coat has reached the "tack-free" stage. This is when it is still soft enough to take a fingerprint but does not adhere to the finger when touched. (For safety, wear a rubber glove when touch-testing curing epoxy.)

No matter what barrier coat system is used, follow the instructions with regard to the final cure. Most systems need to cure fully before being overcoated with antifouling paint. A few should be painted before final cure is reached.

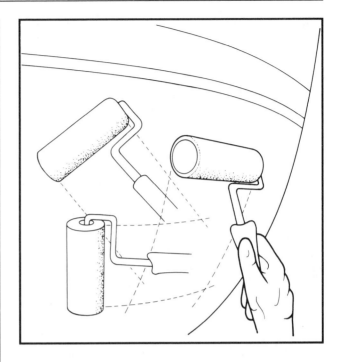

Application of a barrier coat system is the final step in repairing a serious case of osmotic blisters. A paint roller is the most efficient way to apply the barrier coat materials. Follow application instructions for the particular barrier system.

Random Blisters (Any Cause)

Some boats have only a few random blisters. They may be of osmotic origin or they may have been air bubbles trapped between the gel coat and underlying laminate during construction. Fixing random blisters seldom requires complete peeling of the bottom gel coat. A localized repair using epoxy materials should do the job. If there are any doubts as to the nature of the blistering, consult a reputable marine surveyor.

Random blisters are generally treated in the same manner as large blister craters described above. The blister is opened with a grinder until all damaged material is removed. Carefully cut back to the good fiberglass underlying the blister and no farther. Scrub out the blister with a brush and plenty of fresh water, then let the boat dry at least forty-eight hours. If working only on weekends, wash out the blister on Sunday afternoon and let the boat dry all week. The drier the laminate, the better the final repair.

With the WEST System, wet out the blister cavities with unthickened WEST epoxy resin. Allow it to partially cure before making a second application of resin thickened to the consistency of putty. This two-step process is designed to insure good bonding between the fiberglass laminate and the epoxy repair.

Experience has shown that polyester putty should not be used for underwater blisters where the repairs will be covered with antifouling paint. Polyester resins will not cure if exposed to air, and so they are mixed with a waxy substance that migrates to the surface during curing. This wax seals the surface against the air, allowing the putty to cure properly. This wax also prevents paint from adhering properly.

Repainting the Bottom

Antifouling paint goes on after the epoxy putty and barrier coats have cured. Before applying paint, be sure to read and follow the surface-preparation instructions that come with any barrier coat products. Improper preparation of the barrier coat is sure to result in bottom-paint failure. Every third or fourth season it pays to remove the old bottom paint to inspect the barrier coat. Some manufacturers suggest renewing the barrier at regular intervals for maximum protection. If a multi-part

An electric drill motor equipped with a burr cutter can be used to open osmotic and other types of bottom blisters. Great care is needed to control the depth of cut. All blistered material must be removed without doing serious damage to the surrounding laminate. Safety goggles, a respirator (for dust), and gloves should be worn.

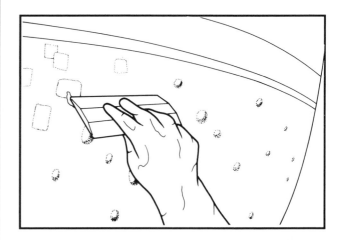

Fill blister craters with an epoxy putty after they have been allowed to dry completely. The best tool for smoothing the putty is a flexible plastic trowel similar to those used in auto body work. It may take several applications to fill deep craters in places where gravity would cause a single filling to sag or fall out.

barrier coat was used to protect the bottom, spot repairs require rebuilding the same layers over any patches.

Sanding begins once the putty in the blister craters has fully cured. Hand sanding is satisfactory for one blister or two, but a serious case of "boat pox" will require an air- or electric-powered dual-action sander. The goal is to fair the patches into the overall shape of the hull.

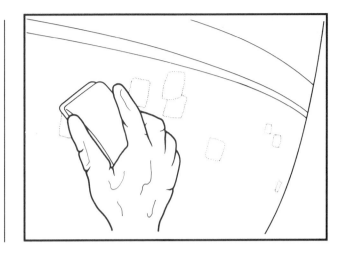

PREVENTING OSMOTIC BLISTERS ON NEW BOATS

Time: Varies with materials.

Materials: Epoxy resin coatings, solvents, rags, disposable gloves, short-nap roller covers, disposable brushes, dewaxing solvents.

Tools: Mixing buckets, roller frames, safety goggles.

Safety: Chemical protection from epoxy resins and solvents; dust protection if sanding is required.

The permeability of fiberglass allows water to migrate inside the laminate of the hull. This permeability is directly linked to osmotic blistering. All current blister prevention techniques revolve around blocking water from entering the laminate. This is most often done by applying several layers of epoxy resin materials (clear or tar) to the area of the boat below the waterline. Epoxies are used for their high resistance to water and their ability to bond tightly with polyester resins commonly used in fiberglass boats.

A new boat should not require gel coat peeling usually done on older boats with severe blistering. The critical factor with a new boat is to remove the residual mold release agent with a commercial de-waxing agent. This may be followed by a light sanding to break up the gel coat gloss. Actual blister protection comes from the application of several layers of epoxy barrier coat material. Choose one of the barrier coat systems and follow instructions to the letter. Any deviation from the instructions may lead to unpredictable results.

Barrier Coat Products

Pettit All-Temp Epoxy Undercoater: This product is white in color, so it can be used under any color antifouling paint. It dries fast, even in cold weather. Its high solids content makes it a good choice for fairing metal keels or smoothing crazed or porous gel coat above the waterline.

Interlux InterProtect: This is a two-part system. New hulls in good condition may be coated with just four or five coats of InterProtect 2000. Hulls with blistering problems require two coats of 1000 Base Coat followed by four or five coats of InterProtect 2000.

WEST System: This is a multi-part system of epoxy resins, fillers, and additives designed for a variety of boat repairs. An initial coating of resin is followed by at least five additional coats mixed with 422 Barrier Coat Additive.

Ordinary masking tape should not be used with epoxies, which will penetrate the paper backing and "glue" it to the hull. Instead, use black plastic electrician's tape. Remove the tape immediately after application of the final coat or at the end of the working day.

Epoxies are messy materials. Uncured epoxy resins can be removed from tools with either acetone or the thinner/reducer specified by the product manufacturer. Avoid uncured epoxy on unprotected skin as it may cause a mild reaction. Always work with good ventilation and wear a respirator if recommended by the product manufacturer.

PRO TIP

A waterless hand cleaner of the type used by auto mechanics does a good job of removing uncured epoxy resin from hands and tools. GoJo brand cleaner is the one preferred by professionals. It works well on wet epoxy but will not soften cured resin.

APPLYING THE BOOT STRIPE

Time: One hour per 25 feet of waterline length.

Materials: Paint or tape, dewaxing agent, fine sandpaper, masking tape, paint thinner, rags, disposable gloves.

Tools: Craft knife or paint brush.

Safety: Paint and chemical protection. Keep sharp tools away from children.

Boot toppings, or boot stripes, are cosmetic bands of accent color that encircle the hull just above the waterline. The boot stripe is always painted on wooden boats. Some fiberglass boat manufacturers mold the color into the gel coat, although most builders use less expensive vinyl tape stripes. Molded colors last the lifespan of the gel coat, but painted and vinyl tape stripes become somewhat bedraggled over time and need renewing.

To be aesthetically correct, the boot stripe should precisely follow the boat's waterline. It should never swoop upward in the bow along a chine or plank lap. Finding the exact waterline on a new boat can be frustrating for the uninitiated. Look for inscribed lines or dimples in the gel coat. If there are none, there is no easy way to calculate the waterline. Instead, take the lazy way and launch the boat for a week and let nature take its course. After a few days there will be a perfect waterline marked by dirt and scum. Haul the boat and use the scum line as a guide for marking the location of the boot stripe.

The bottom of the boot stripe should be about an inch above the boat's actual waterline. The top-side color of the hull can show through this inch, or antifouling paint can be applied right up to the stripe. A properly applied stripe appears to be of uniform width, but it's actually slightly wider at the bow and narrower amidships. On boats with counter sterns (such as most sailboats), the stripe will be much wider aft as well. Although the width changes, the stripe *appears* to be of uniform width to an observer from the side of the boat.

Water-Level the Stripe

The necessary width variations can be calculated, but it's a lot easier to use a water level instead. A water level consists of two clear tubes connected by a length of hose. The hose is filled with water so that water shows in both clear tubes. Commercial water levels can be purchased, but it's simple enough to concoct one in the average home workshop out of a garden hose and a couple of lengths of clear plastic tubing.

One clear tube is taped to the hull amidships so that the water level in it is exactly at the top of the boot stripe. The other clear tube is moved fore and aft as a guide for marking the top of the stripe. Position the tube against the hull and make a pencil mark at the level of water. Thanks to hydraulics, the water level in the moving tube will be exactly the same as in the stationary tube taped to the hull. Naturally, this system of marking the top of the boot stripe will only work if the hull has been properly leveled in its cradle.

Tape Stripes

Vinyl striping tape comes in a variety of widths from ¾ inch to 4 inches. Colors available to the public tend to be the primary reds, blues, and greens. Choose a color to accent the coloration of the boat. The width of the tape should be equal to the width of the boot stripe amidships. To avoid color mismatches, get enough tape for the entire job at one store. There are slight color variations from batch to batch, just as with knitting yarn.

Start at the bow of sailboats and at the stern of powerboats, as these are the areas with the least curve. Peel the paper backing off about 6 inches of tape. Apply this peeled section carefully to the hull on the waterline marks and rub it down firmly. The stripe is now "anchored" to the hull. The person applying the tape should walk backwards away from the anchor, peeling the backing with one hand while applying tension to the tape with the other. Don't stretch the tape, just pull it taut. Align the tape with guide marks and let it "grab" the hull by itself. Work with 3-to-5-foot lengths of tape.

Don't worry if the tape "grabs" wrong. It will come away without much fuss until it has been firmly rubbed down. Gently pull the tape off the hull and relocate it. Once the position is absolutely correct, a helper should firmly rub down the tape. Air bubbles are inevitable, but most can be worked to the edge of the tape with finger pressure. An oc-

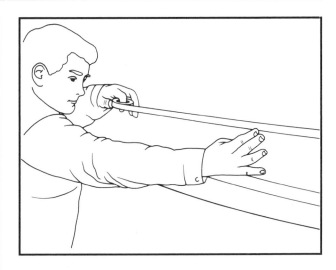

Sight along the boot stripe when applying vinyl accent tape to insure that it is running straight along the hull. One hand holds the tape roll while the other smooths the tape to the hull. The stripe should run in a straight line from bow to stern.

casional bubble will resist moving. Lance it with the tip of a sharp knife and rub down the tape. Once rubbed down, the lance mark can't be seen.

Tape can be joined by overlapping the old with the new. Use a very sharp knife to carefully cut through both layers without cutting into the gel coat. Peel off the upper scrap and toss it away. Then temporarily peel up the top layer so the scrap piece beneath it can be pulled off the hull and discarded. Lay down the upper layer so it butts against the lower layer. The cut lines should match perfectly with no gaps or overlaps. This technique can be used for lengthening the tape horizontally or for adding vertical width at the bow and stern.

Some tape stripes have a clear protective coating that must be removed after application. Use a fingernail to scratch up the coating at one end of the tape. Peel up about 2 inches clear coating and then fold it back over the top of the stripe. Pull on this tab of coating while walking along the hull, keeping a sharp bend in the coating where it comes away from the tape.

Tape stripes should be allowed at least forty-eight hours to bond to the hull before launching, especially on high-speed powerboats.

Painted Stripes

Paint affords you the widest choice of boot stripe colors. Alkyd enamels are the least expensive. Their shorter lifespan is not a problem because boot stripes usually need yearly touchup or renewal. One-part polyurethane paints retain their gloss longer, but need the same annual attention to nicks and scrapes. Two-part polyurethanes are definitely overkill, both in terms of cost and difficulty of application.

Mold release agent should be removed from the boot stripe area with dewaxing agent to insure the paint will adhere properly. Since the agent will wash away pencil marks, dewax *before* marking the location of the stripe. Apply double layers of ordinary masking tape to outline the top and bottom of the boot stripe, one layer on top of the other. Two layers will give good protection to the gel coat while you are dry sanding the stripe area with 220 paper.

Remove the two protective layers of ordinary masking tape after sanding and replace them with 3M's Fine Line masking tape to delineate the top and bottom of the stripe. Wipe down the area to be painted with a dry cloth to remove any dust and apply the paint according to the instructions. Initial applications usually require two coats for full color and gloss. Sanding between coats won't be necessary *only* if the second coat is applied as soon as the first one dries tack-free. Check the label on

Masking tape should be applied above and below the boot stripe before applying paint. Using full inch-wide tape will prevent minor slips of the brush from getting onto the hull or bottom paint. All masking tape should be removed immediately upon completion of the painting.

the paint for exact instructions regarding application of the second coat.

Antifouling Protection

Boot stripes are theoretically out of the water, but they often suffer from marine growth and dirty water. One way to avoid some of these problems is to apply antifouling wax to the boot stripe. This wax can be applied directly over new tape stripes. Application over new paint should be delayed a week until it has thoroughly dried and hardened. Antifouling wax is not as good as antifouling paint, but it provides a measure of protection.

SPIFFING UP TIRED GEL COAT

Time: One hour per 40 square feet of hull.

Materials: Rubbing compound, wax, polish, cleaner.

Tools: Power buffer.

Safety: Power tool safety.

People love to build things out of the wrong materials. Take boats, for instance. Slick, shiny hulls are constantly being attacked by barnacle-encrusted pilings, concrete quays, ultraviolet sunlight and gritty fenders. No wonder gel coats get dull and scratched after only a few seasons. A more practical species than humans would build boats out of hard black rubber or some other material that doesn't show damage. Of course, dull black boats would be ugly beyond imagination. Perhaps there are times when practicality should take a back seat to beauty.

Gel coat maintenance requires some understanding of what it is—and what it is not. Gel coat serves much the same function as paint on a wooden boat: appearance and protection. It also helps keep water and other injurious chemicals out of the underlying fiberglass laminate. While gel coat can be colorful, it's only moderately successful at the more important job of protecting the boat. Despite an impervious appearance, it is actually quite porous and will absorb water, dirt, and many chemicals. Ultraviolet light from the sun bakes the life out of gel coat and causes chalking.

Don't despair—with proper care and feeding, gel coat can be helped to battle its enemies. The exterior of any boat can stay looking good almost indefinitely. That's the good news. The bad news is that taking proper care of gel coat is almost as much physical labor as sanding and painting a wooden boat. And you believed all that "no maintenance" stuff in the sales literature!

The Washdown

Gel coat maintenance starts with a thorough washdown using mild soap and plenty of clean, fresh, rinse water. An excellent boat wash comes from an unlikely source, the Pettit Paint Company. Now sold under the name Meaner Cleaner, this purple liquid cleans fiberglass and just about everything else. Sudbury's Boat Zoap is another good choice. There are also good cleaning products available at the local super market. Biodegradable dishwashing detergent works well on fiberglass and is less expensive than most of the stuff sold by boat stores.

Soap and a soft-bristled nylon brush should remove about 99 percent of the dirt and grime. A patchwork of serious stains that doesn't wash off may be a sign that the gel coat is "dead" and needs to be either recoated or painted. Some types of dirt can stain even brand-new gel coats.

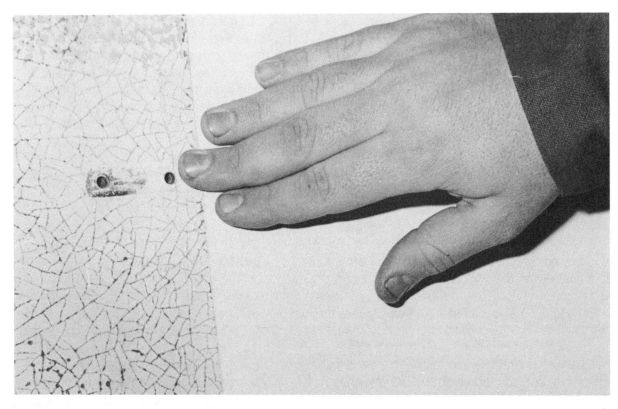

Dramatic improvement in the appearance of gel coat is possible with professional refinishing. The alligator appearance shown here was attacked in a series of steps. The cracks were first filled with matching gel coat. Then, the entire bottom was wet sanded. The final step was power buffing using a series of rubbing compounds followed by a coat of wax.

A thorough scrubbing with a mild soap and a special soft brush made for the job is always the first step in gel coat maintenance. Note that the brush can be attached to a long handle, making it easy to scrub the deck while standing upright. Cleaners that contain grit should be used only as a last resort, as they will eventually dull the gel coat.

Oil, rust, and exhaust gasses are all members of this stain gang.

Stain Removers

Special stain removing products are available. Calahan's FSR (Fiberglass Stain Remover) is a blue gel that stays put on top of the stain while it works. Y-10 is a similar product. Stain removers use chemicals, abrasives, or a combination of the two to get out the discoloration. Read and follow the directions, especially any safety precautions.

Household cleaners can be used on exceptionally dirty decks or along the waterline. Soft Scrub and Barkeeper's Friend are two such products. These household cleaners say they don't scratch, but it would be closer to the truth to say that they don't make big scratches. No matter how mild, any abrasive cleaner will eventually dull gel coat.

Cleaners containing grit should be used sparingly and only on areas that really need extra cleaning power. One scrubbing in the spring and additional occasional washings on tough dirt during the season are not likely to cause any serious problems. Excessive use of abrasive cleaners, however, will hasten the day when the boat needs an expensive cosmetic job.

Restoring Gel Color

Fading color is the first sign that gel coat is beginning to weather. Reds fade first. Blues and greens seem to resist longer. A wide variety of products designed to restore faded gel coats is available under the generic term "color restorers." Most contain petroleum distillates or similar chemicals that soak into the porous gel coat and fill the microscopic empty spaces created by weathering. The result is a darker, richer color.

Some color-restoring products may also contain an extremely mild rubbing compound to remove minute amounts of the most weathered gel coat from the top surface. Improvement will be very short-lived if the surface of the gel coat is not properly sealed to prevent the color-restoring chemicals from evaporating out of the porous gel coat.

Color restorers are almost mandatory on older boats. They are not needed or recommended on new boats or on boats that do not exhibit signs of chalking or fading.

Sealing the Surface

Sealing is the final step in gel coat maintenance. It is done either with a liquid polish or with a paste wax. Companies that make color restorers also produce gel coat sealers. The best advice is to use companion products intended to work together. Mixing brands probably won't do any harm, but may not give the long-lasting results desired.

Fifteen years ago there was considerable debate over whether liquid polishes would last as long as traditional paste wax products. In the beginning, most liquids weren't as good, but that is no longer true. Liquid products have caught up to and even surpassed the longevity of paste waxes. Carnauba wax products, with their tedious buffing, are losing popularity to one-step liquid polishes. Liquids are easier to apply and easier to buff out.

Whatever product is used, *follow the instructions*. Polishes aren't particularly rough on hands, but they do get under fingernails and into the ridges of knuckles. It can take two or three washings to get the residue off. Rubber gloves are the obvious solution. Eye protection is always a good idea too, but especially for wearers of contact lenses. Dried polish produces dust that is almost certain to get into eyes.

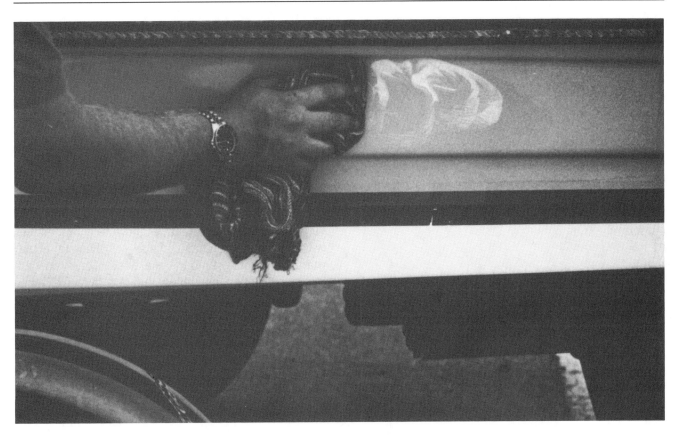

Liquid polish is applied with a soft applicator such as a sponge or rag. Once it has dried to a light haze, it is buffed off with an old bath towel or other soft cloth. Mechanical buffing is not necessary.

Let the chemicals in the polish do the work. Once the gel coat is clean, allow the polish to dry to a white powder-like state. Then buff with a soft cloth, turning often. From time to time, shake out the buffing rag to get rid of powder buildup. Work the rag in straight lines parallel to the waterline to avoid annoying swirl marks in the finished job.

Mechanical buffing improves the appearance of the finished job and there is anecdotal evidence that mechanically buffed wax actually lasts a bit longer. Use a low- or medium-speed buffer with a bonnet designed for fiberglass. Stop at regular intervals to remove any dried wax or polish that has built up in the bonnet. (Dried bits of polish in the bonnet act like grinding stones against the gel coat.) Work in big motions. Never let the spinning buffer rest in one spot.

Two Coats Are Better

A second coat of sealer improves the longevity of polish or wax. Wait a week or so for the first coat to fully harden before applying the second. This waiting period is more important for liquid polishes than for paste waxes, because the liquids tend to be their own solvents. A "new" layer of polish can be removed by the second coat, while an "old" layer (older by a week) is usually not as greatly affected.

Even the most careful worker will leave behind a fine dust of dried wax or cleaner after the rubout. Use an old bath towel to wipe this dust off the hull. Then stand back, pop the top of a cool one, and admire the gleaming gel coat.

Nonskid Areas

Safety requires that nonskid areas remain just that, *nonskid*. This raises one of the great problems in fiberglass boat maintenance. Polishing or waxing nonskid areas is not recommended because it makes these areas slippery. Also, it's nearly impossible to get dried wax or polish residue out of the nonskid pattern. Yet, decks (where nonskid areas are located) suffer the worst weathering from ultraviolet sunlight because they are horizontal. Nonskid areas need all the protection they can get from harsh sunlight, despite the fact that protection can be a safety hazard. There are no easy answers to this dilemma.

New from Star brite is Non-Skid Deck Cleaner/Protector. Directions call for hosing down the deck with fresh water, then spreading this new cleaner with a deck brush. Let it sit for two to three minutes. According to the manufacturer, a special chelating action dissolves the dirt. After a quick scrubbing, the cleaner is hosed off the deck with fresh water. Star brite claims this product leaves behind a protective coating that resists gel coat weathering.

REPAIRING MINOR GEL COAT DAMAGE

Time: Varies with job. Plan minimum of one hour, plus sanding and buffing.

Materials: Gel coat, thickening agent, plastic wrap, masking tape, acetone, rags, wet and dry sandpaper, buffing compound.

Tools: Disposable artist's brush, putty knife, sanding block, electric buffer.

Safety: Hand and eye protection from resin, catalyst, and acetone. Fire safety precautions when using acetone. Electric tool safety.

Scrapes and scratches are inevitable. Minor insults to the gel coat can be removed with rubbing compound, but there will always be damage that requires you to repair the gel coat rather than just buff it. Large scratches or serious damage are best left to the professional. Small scratches, however, can be repaired by anyone moderately handy with tools.

The first problem is deciding which cracks to repair. Some extremely small "spider cracks" are probably best left alone. Repairs are possible, but the results may be more objectionable than hairline cracks. Serious scratches more than ⅛ inch wide or 3 to 4 inches long are best handed over to a professional. Somewhere between these two extremes lie the scratches, dents, and dings that can be fixed by the boat owner.

Unthickened gel coat has the consistency of latex house paint. It "bridges" extremely narrow cracks instead of flowing into and filling them. For this reason, very small cracks must be "opened up" a bit with the edge of a sharp tool. Be careful not to do more damage, especially if the tool slips out of the scratch.

Use a sharp knife point to probe all of the edges of the crack for loose gel coat. Any chips still adhering to the hull must be popped free. Once the crack is opened and cleaned, let the boat dry overnight (or longer) to eliminate moisture trapped in the underlying laminate. (If the boat is outdoors, protect the scratch from morning dew.)

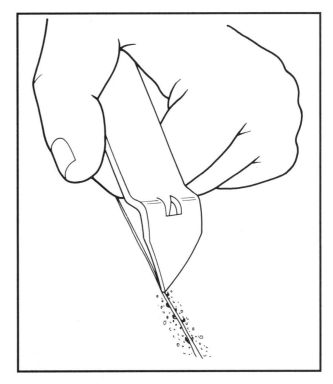

Small gel coat scratches must be opened before they can be repaired properly. Use any sharp tool so long as it can be carefully controlled, since if it skips, the sharp edge will do more damage.

Deep Gouges or Scrapes

Deep gouges can be filled with multiple layers of gel coat, but this is time-consuming. A better solution is to use polyester auto body filler to raise the bottom of the gouge up nearly to the level of the surrounding gel coat. *Nearly* is the key word. The gouge must still be a depression below the surrounding surface or it will be impossible to cover it with color-matched gel coat. If the putty is brought to the level of the surrounding surface, the patch will always show through when the new gel coat is sanded fair with the rest of the hull.

Shallow gouges can be filled from top to bottom with color-matched gel coat paste. White paste gel coat is available for this purpose. Colors are created by adding appropriate tinting materials to produce an exact color match. If paste gel coat is not

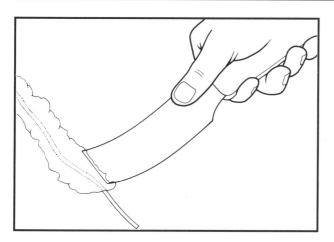

Gel coat paste can be troweled into the open crack with a flexible putty knife. Draw the knife across the crack to insure that it is filled completely. Wet gel coat in the crack should stand proud above the surrounding surface, as it will shrink as it cures.

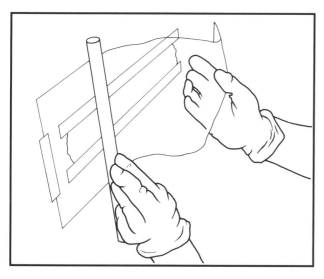

Air-inhibited gel coat will not cure if exposed to air. The solution is to cover it with a layer of plastic kitchen wrap. Press the wrap carefully against the wet gel coat to drive out any air bubbles. Smoothing the wrap also achieves a shiny, ready-to-sand surface when the resin cures. Hold the wrap in position with masking tape.

available, it can be made on the job by adding an appropriate thickening agent to liquid gel coat. Ground talcum (soapstone) is often used by professionals, but most low-density fillers will work. Paste gel coat is also useful for filling cracks on vertical, or nearly vertical, surfaces, where gravity causes regular gel coat to drip out.

PRO TIP

Deep gouges in gel coat can be filled with polyester putty or epoxy mending materials. Epoxy putties are stronger, but some experts say that polyester putty sticks a bit better to gel coat (a polyester resin). Special marine-grade polyester putties are advised. If these are not available, polyester auto body filler may be substituted.

Improperly catalyzed polyester resins are a major cause of do-it-yourself repair failures. Use exactly the amount of catalyst specified for the batch being mixed. Careful measurements are required. (Always wear eye protection when handling catalysts.) Thoroughly mix the catalyst into the resin. There is no way to visually check that the catalyst is evenly dispersed throughout the resin, so vigorous mixing is the only insurance that the entire batch is catalyzed. Extra mixing is always advised with thickened gel coat or gel coat putty.

Liquid gel coat can be applied with a disposable brush or by spraying. Brushing is the safest method, since spraying requires a NIOSH-approved respirator. Paste gel coat is best applied with a slightly flexible putty knife. It is neither necessary nor particularly advised to build up the entire scratch in one application. Several thin coats will result in a better repair. The final coat should build the surface of the scratch *slightly higher* than the surrounding surface because gel coat shrinks as it cures.

Spraying gel coat does not require expensive equipment. Go to the neighborhood auto paint store and ask for a Pre Val Sprayer. This is a self-contained spray can that can be filled with any kind of paint or gel coat. Use acetone to thin the color-matched gel coat to the consistency of milk. Add approximately fifteen drops of catalyst per ounce of thinned gel coat. Test spray some gel coat onto a piece of cardboard to get the "feel" of the sprayer. Be sure to wear a respirator.

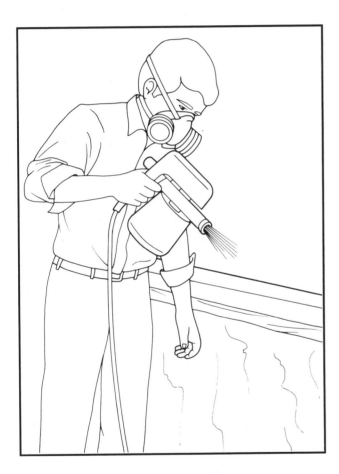

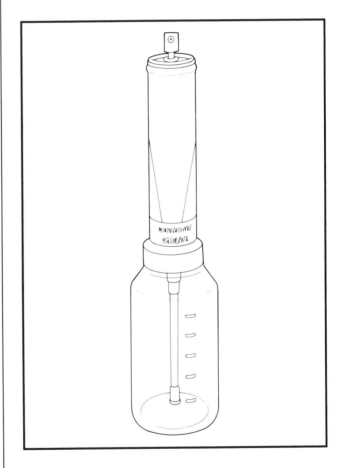

Gel coat can be applied to large areas with an airless spray gun. However, it is a difficult technique to learn, and an organic-chemical respirator is required for safety. Spraying should be attempted only by people familiar with the technique.

Small areas can be recoated with gel coat using a Pre Val spray bottle. Available through auto parts stores, this bottle is really just an aerosol spray can that can be filled with anything from oil paint to fiberglass gel coat. Pre Val spray bottles can be cleaned and reused, but they are inexpensive enough to be tossed out when the job is done.

Mist on the first coat and wait a few minutes before applying the second. Two coats should be enough, although a third may be applied. Several thin coats applied about five minutes apart are less likely to sag and run than one thick coat. If additional coats are applied before the first one cures, it is not necessary to dewax or sand before recoating. Heat lamps can be used to make wet gel coat "kick" faster, but avoid overheating fiberglass materials. Polyester resins are easily deformed by excessive heat. Warming the surface to no more than 85 degrees should be sufficient to speed the chemical reaction without damage.

Air-Curing Resins

Polyester gel coat resins and putties sold for amateur repairs will cure when exposed to air. Professional gel coat (such as the color-matched material shipped with the boat from the factory) will *not* cure properly when exposed to air. Professional materials that are exposed to air while curing will remain dull and sticky like flypaper. This feature allows additional coats to be applied without sanding or dewaxing. Such professional resins are called "air-inhibited." (A hard cure of the final layer can be obtained by covering the patch tightly with plastic wrap from the kitchen. Smooth the wrap tightly over the wet gel coat with light pressure to eliminate any trapped air. Seal the edges of the wrap with masking tape.)

Resins that cure hard when exposed to air contain dissolved wax that "floats" to the surface during curing. This wax forms a microscopic barrier against the air. Additional coats cannot be applied unless the wax barrier is removed by wiping with acetone and sanding lightly with 220 grit paper. Failure to remove the wax will prevent additional coats from adhering to the repair.

Gel coat should be allowed to cure for at least

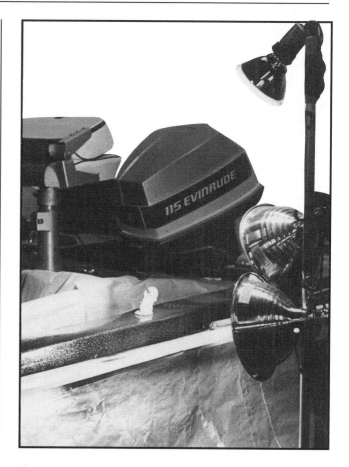

Heat lamps can be used to make polyester resins "kick" faster, but great caution is necessary. The lamps must be far enough away from the boat so that they only warm the surface without getting it hot. Too much heat can cause cured polyester resin to soften or distort.

twenty-four hours before attempting any final finishing. Following the instructions in Chapter 2 ("Wet Sanding Gel Coat," page 49), wet sand until the new gel coat is smooth and fair with the surrounding surface. Work up through the grits to at least 1,200. Follow wet sanding with light buffing using a very mild compound.

Color Matching

Boats are often shipped from the factory with a small jar of color-matched gel coat from the batch used to build the boat. This is supposed to eliminate the frustrating procedure of color matching gel coat repairs. On a brand-new boat, factory-supplied gel coat will match perfectly, but this happy situation is short-lived. Weathering of the hull starts immediately after the boat leaves the factory. Gel coat will have changed color noticeably after just half a season in harsh sunlight. Factory gel coat will be close to the actual color of the hull, but there'll be a discernible difference. Three or four years down the road, factory gel coat may be a worse match than locally mixed gel coat prepared by someone with a good "color eye."

Professionals use a material called "patching additive" to blend a repaired area into the rest of the hull. The technique takes a while to acquire, so it isn't suggested for the amateur. Essentially, patching additive is just crystal-clear gel coat. It is mixed with the regular gel coat to thin out the color saturation. This allows an expert with a spray gun to gradually blend the new color into the old.

Sanding and Buffing

Wet sanding and buffing may or *may not* be necessary to complete the repair. If the cured gel coat blends well with its surroundings and doesn't draw attention to itself, quit while you're ahead. It is extremely easy to make a good job look bad by over-sanding and buffing. However, if the new gel coat stands proud above the surrounding area, or if there is a dull area of overspray surrounding the patch, some sanding and buffing will be needed.

Wet sanding is the best way to level a patch into the surrounding area. Start with a grit no rougher than 440. Move down to 220 grit only if absolutely necessary. Work with long, straight strokes and keep the surface lubricated with water (see page 49). Work up through the grits, finishing up with 1,200 grit. This should bring the patch to a high state of gloss.

Mechanical buffing is the final—and most dangerous—step. Use a medium or fine cut rubbing compound and work with light pressure on the buffing wheel. Clean the buffing pad often to prevent buildup of hard particles of compound. This step can also be done without a machine. It takes longer, but is less likely to burn through the new gel coat. (See the section on "Rubbing Out Faded Hulls," page 50.)

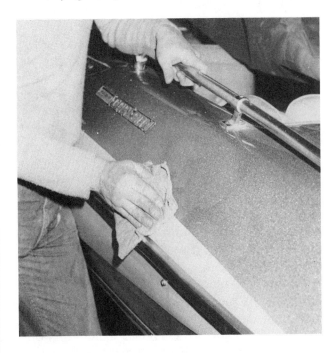

Rubbing compound can be used effectively by hand to give a final buff and polish to a repair. Hand rubbing is less likely to cause gel coat "burn-through" or other damage than polishing with a machine. Straight horizontal or vertical strokes should be used in place of circular rubbing to avoid swirl marks.

REPLACING SACRIFICIAL ZINC ANODES

Time: Fifteen to thirty minutes per zinc.
Materials: New zincs, possibly mounting hardware.
Tools: Screwdriver or wrench, pry bar.
Safety: Hand tool safety.

A crude electric battery is created whenever two dissimilar metals are immersed in an electrolytic solution. Current flow causes the less noble of these two metals to deteriorate in a process known as "galvanic corrosion." Modern boats expose a mixture of bronze, stainless steel, Monel, and aluminum to the water. These underwater parts are electrically connected either through a bonding system or the boat's electrical system, thus setting up a perfect situation for galvanic corrosion. Aluminum is particularly vulnerable, but bronze propellers and struts also have been turned into metallic "Swiss cheese" by this type of corrosion.

Protecting underwater metals is the job of so-called sacrificial zinc anodes. They may be installed on the rudder, the propeller shaft, propeller struts or the hull itself. Outboard motors and outdrive lower units also have sacrificial zincs to protect their vulnerable aluminum gearboxes. As their name implies, zinc anodes sacrifice themselves to protect the expensive underwater hardware. The lifespan of zincs depends upon the amount of dissimilar metal, its placement, and the type of water.

Some zincs need replacement twice a season while others may last a decade.

Replacing zincs should involve nothing more complex than unfastening the old and tightening down the new. Of course, anywhere there's corrosion there are reluctant bolts and screws. Getting old zincs off can be a three-curse job. More often than not, the old fasteners must be destroyed in the process.

Installation is the reverse. Care must be taken to be sure the new zinc is electrically connected to the material that it protects. This connection was made originally by the boat builder when the first zinc anodes were installed. Connecting a new anode should present no unusual problems, especially when zincs are mounted directly onto metal parts. The metal to be protected should be sanded bright with 150 grit sandpaper to insure a good connection.

Outboard and I-O lower units require special zincs available through authorized dealers. Some units have blocks of zinc that bolt to the vertical leg. On other units the trim tab below the anticavitation plate serves double duty as a zinc.

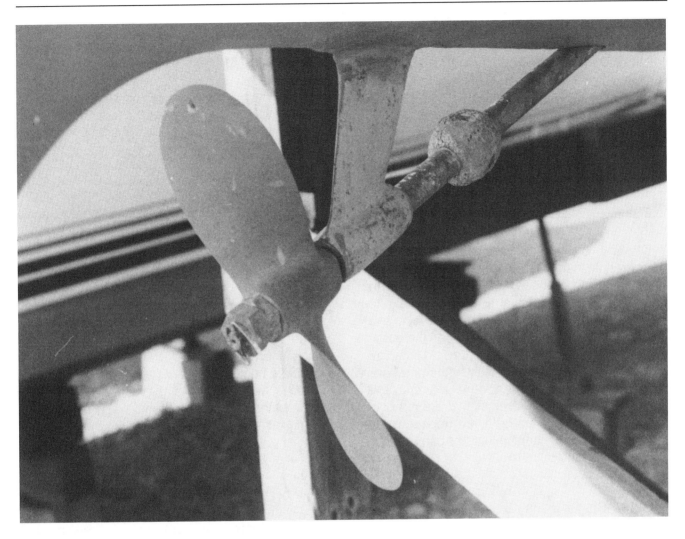

WARNING

Sacrificial zinc protection is vital to the boat's health. If you have any doubts about your ability to replace zincs, refer this task to a professional. Failure to protect underwater gear can lead to expensive repairs.

Sacrificial zincs are used to protect shafts and propellers from corrosion. Zincs for this purpose are usually egg-shaped collars that fit on the shafts. Mounting screws hold the zincs in position. Tapping a zinc tells a lot about its health: A zinc that needs replacement will produce a shower of particles when hit sharply.

MAINTAINING SEA COCKS AND VALVES

Time: Thirty minutes per sea cock.

Materials: Waterproof grease.

Tools: Wrench.

Safety: Hand tool safety. This job should be done with the boat out of the water.

Nautical dictionaries call any valve on a through-hull fitting below the waterline a "sea cock." The job of these valves is to shut off the incoming flow of sea water to allow maintenance of the boat's internal plumbing. Prudence says that sea cocks should be closed when the boat is left unattended for extended periods of time. However, most owners neglect this safety procedure simply because the number of valves has proliferated on modern craft. Valves that are not operated regularly often corrode or "freeze" in the open position. Regular maintenance can keep sea cocks functioning smoothly.

Tapered-Plug Valves

Traditional sea cocks consist of a tapered bronze plug inside a bronze body. Because it is tapered, the plug fits tightly into the body of the valve and yet will turn easily. A hole in the plug allows water to flow through the valve when it is lined up with the inlet and outlet. A quarter-turn of the handle rotates this hole at right angles to the inlet and outlet, effectively blocking the flow of water.

Maintenance of tapered-plug sea cocks starts with removing the plug from the valve body. Obviously, this can only be done with the boat out of the water. A nut on the end opposite to the handle holds the plug in place. Loosening this nut allows the plug to be pulled sideways out of the body. Inspect the plug for signs of unusual wear or for rough spots, which can be removed with emery paper. Carefully probe the inside of the plug body to find any rough spots. Again, emery paper should smooth things out.

Coat the plug with a thin layer of waterproof grease and reassemble the valve. The nut should be tightened to the point where the handle moves against mild resistance and remains where it is positioned. Better to have a trickle of water than to have the nut so tight that the handle won't move. After launching, check the sea cock to make sure that water is not weeping around the plug. A slight snugging on the nut should end any weeping without making the plug so tight that it can't be rotated with the handle. The sea cock must turn without force. Survival could depend on being able to close it in a hurry.

Bronze sea cocks have a drain plug in the side of the body. This plug should be removed once a year and the threads coated with waterproof grease. Retighten the drain plug so that it won't leak water and so that engine vibrations won't cause it to come loose.

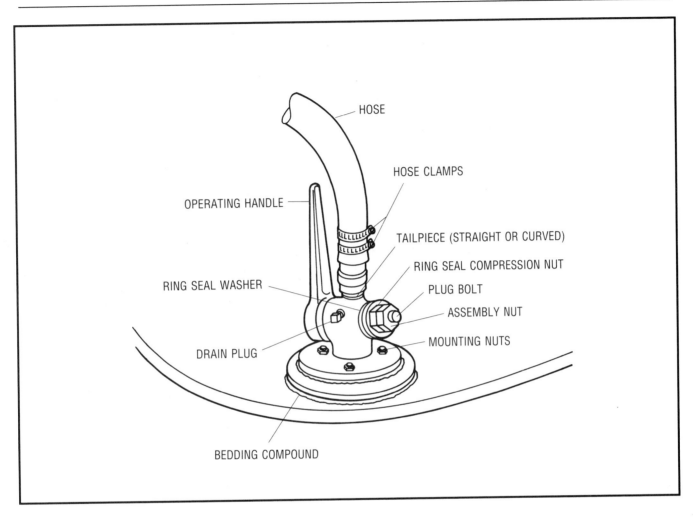

HOSE

HOSE CLAMPS

OPERATING HANDLE

TAILPIECE (STRAIGHT OR CURVED)

RING SEAL COMPRESSION NUT

RING SEAL WASHER

PLUG BOLT

ASSEMBLY NUT

DRAIN PLUG

MOUNTING NUTS

BEDDING COMPOUND

Rubber Plug Valves

Some valves replace the tapered metal plug with one made out of synthetic rubber. This type of valve should be disassembled once each season for cleaning and inspection. Worn plugs should be replaced to restore the valve's original performance. Adjust the reassembled valve so that the handle moves smoothly. This type of valve is not supposed to need lubrication. If it is still difficult to move after servicing, try vegetable cooking oil as a lubricant.

Ball and Nonmetallic Sea Cocks

Recent years have seen a proliferation of metal ball valves used as sea cocks. Ball valves may be housed in traditional bronze bodies, or they may be made out of a tough space-age plastic. Ball valves come to boating by way of the chemical industry, where they have proven to be maintenance-free. Annual disassembly and greasing is not required. Regular "exercise" is the only maintenance that should be necessary. Open and close ball valves a couple of times each month during the season to be sure they are working smoothly. Sticky valves should be replaced.

Regular lubrication of ball valves will prolong their useful life. With the boat out of the water, remove the hose from the valve. Close the valve and pour a small amount of vegetable cooking oil from the galley into the valve body. Open and close the ball valve several times to distribute the oil around the working parts. Replace the hose and tighten the hose clamps.

Hoses and Hose Clamps

While working on the sea cocks it's a good idea to check the hoses attached to them. The rubber should still feel "live" and there should be no unexplained bulges or flat spots. Check to see that all hose clamps are tight and that neither the actuating screw nor the clamp itself has started to corrode. Look at the hose rubber just above and below each clamp. Clamp bands have been known to cut through soft rubber. All hoses on through-hull fittings below the waterline must be double clamped.

Soft Tapered Wooden Plugs

A tapered wooden plug should be located next to each sea cock. This plug should be sized according to the diameter of the through-hull fitting. In an emergency, the plug can be hammered into the sea cock body to shut off the incoming flow of water. One way to keep wood plugs handy is to attach them to their respective sea cocks with a short lanyard of nylon cord. Drill a hole in the wide end of the plug for the lanyard. Attach the other end of the nylon cord to the handle of the sea cock.

SELF-STICK NUMBERS AND LETTERS

Time: One minute per letter.

Materials: New letters, dewaxing agent, rags.

Tools: Heat gun.

Safety: Electric tool safety; care using heat on fiberglass; chemical safety for dewaxing agent.

Self-stick numbers and letters allow everyone to do a professional-looking job numbering or lettering. The majority of boats displaying state registration numbers use self-stick digits. These letters are ideal for use on fiberglass and they stick well to smooth, well-adhered paint on wood or metal boats. Block letters and numbers are available for displaying state registration numbers on the bow while larger script letters are perfect for names and hailing ports on the stern.

Installing New Letters and Numbers

Self-stick letters and numbers adhere best to gel coat and to paint that has not been waxed or polished. Silicone polishes are notoriously slippery. Rough water has washed registration numbers right off the bows of boats coated with silicone wax. So before installing new letters, it's a good idea to dewax the gel coat. Mineral spirits, acetone, or a commercial dewaxing agent can be used. Of these, mineral spirits and the commercial product are least likely to damage the gel coat. Excessive use of acetone may soften or dull polyester resins. Paint on wooden boats is seldom waxed, but a washdown with clean, mild soap and water is still a good idea.

Draw a horizontal pencil line on the hull indicating the top or bottom alignment of the letters. Let the job decide whether to line up the tops or bottoms of the letters. Since most self-stick numbers are block style and of the same height, a top line works as well as a bottom line. Script letters are not all the same height, so only a bottom line can be used for them.

Peel the backing halfway off the letter. Using the unpeeled section, slide the letter on the hull until it is properly aligned with the baseline. Then burnish down the peeled section. Peel off the rest of the

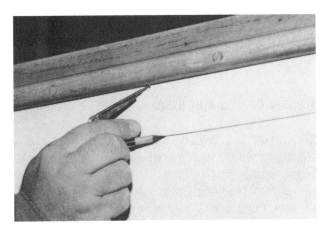

A scribing compass can be used to draw a pencil line on the hull for aligning self-stick numbers. This is possible only when it is desirable that the letters follow the sheer line. Alternatively, a straight wood batten can be held against the hull to guide the scribing compass if the letters are not to follow the sheer line.

Self-stick letters must be carefully aligned on the hull. Remove the paper backing from a portion of the letter, exposing some of the stickum. Holding the unpeeled section of the letter, move it around on the hull until it is properly aligned. Rub down the sticky part of the letter, then remove the rest of the paper backing and rub the entire letter in position.

backing and rub down the remainder of the letter.

Wax or polish protection can be restored to the gel coat right on top of the new letters or numbers.

Removing Old Numbers

Getting old numbers off the hull can be a problem. Scraping with a putty knife or single-edge razor blade works, but it leaves telltale gouges in paint or gel coat. Self-stick letters are easily removed by heating them gently with a heat gun. Heat softens the adhesive so that the putty knife can lift the old letter without endangering the gel coat.

Caution must be observed when using a heat gun around fiberglass. *Excess heat may cause polyester resin to deform, permanently damaging the boat.* Use only enough heat to soften the glue on the letters, no more. An ordinary hair-dryer puts out more than enough heat to get the job done.

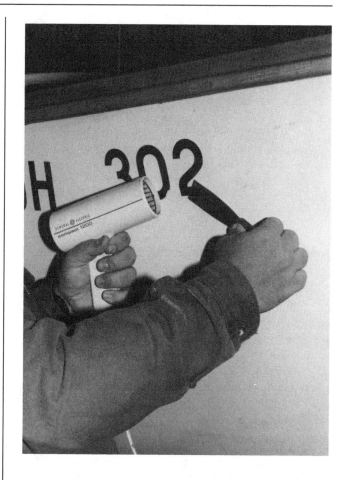

Heat makes removing old self-stick letters easy. An ordinary hair-dryer provides sufficient hot air to soften the glue of a letter or number without damaging the fiberglass hull. Lift the letter with a putty knife. Using heat avoids the need to scrape the old letter off with a razor blade, which always results in unwanted gouges in the gel coat.

CHAPTER 4

THE EXTERIOR

While the hull *is* the boat, it's the exterior appearance that gives the first impression of the craft. A well-maintained appearance bespeaks a seaworthy boat, while scratches, dents, bent rails, and faded gel coat tell a different story. Most maintenance on fiberglass boats is exterior work, such as fixing gel coat cracks and refastening deck hardware. Not all of these jobs are fun. Many require considerable labor. However, generations of owners have discovered that keeping a boat in "Bristol fashion" is its own reward.

REPLACING WORN ANCHOR ROLLERS

Time: Thirty to ninety minutes.

Materials: New roller, stainless-steel cotter pins.

Tools: Pliers, screwdriver, wrench, drift punch, hammer.

Safety: Eye protection when using drift punch and hammer.

The initial step in removing the old anchor roller is to remove the lock nut from the axle bolt. This is most easily done by using an end wrench with one hand and a ratchet handle and socket wrench with the other.

Once the lock nut has been removed, the axle bolt can be taken out of the roller. It may be necessary to strike the bolt with a plastic hammer to loosen it inside of the rubber roller.

Anchor rollers make handling ground tackle so much easier. It's surprising more builders don't include them as standard equipment. Rollers are simple devices with little to go wrong other than deterioration of the roller itself: Exposure to ultraviolet light and salt water may cause the roller to cease turning or to become cracked and brittle.

Replacing a roller is not difficult. Most are mounted on a stainless-steel pin that acts as its axle. This pin is held captive either by stainless-steel cotter pins or aircraft-style locking nuts. The pin should slip out after the retaining devices have been removed. If there has been much corrosion, it may be necessary to drive the pin out with a tool called a "drift" (or "drift punch") and a hammer. Wear safety goggles, and tap carefully to avoid bending or breaking any of the mounting parts.

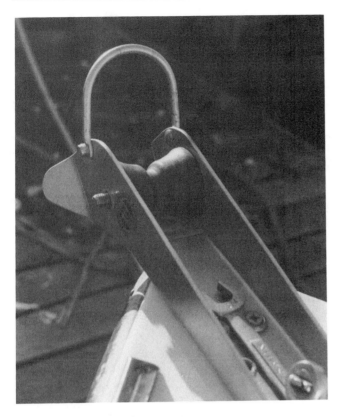

Follow the reverse procedure to install the new roller by pushing the axle bolt back through the metal mounting bracket. Check roller alignment and action before completing the job.

Two wrenches are used to tighten the lock nut on the axle bolt in the final step of anchor roller replacement.

Boat builders sometimes fabricate their own anchor roller assemblies using stock boat trailer rollers. Replacements are easily obtained from stores specializing in trailer boat equipment. Don't buy cheap rubber rollers. Look for more expensive rollers made of sun-resistant, man-made materials. Be sure the axle hole in the roller is the same size as the pin from the boat.

Commercial anchor roller assemblies are used by some builders. These assemblies are also popular with boat owners for do-it-yourself installation. Companies that produce these assemblies also sell replacement rollers. Unfortunately, few chandleries stock them. The best way to obtain the right replacement roller is to contact the manufacturer directly.

FIXING DECK HARDWARE LEAKS

Time: Sixty to ninety minutes.
Materials: Bedding compound or caulking, solvent, rags.
Tools: Screwdriver, wrench, putty knife.
Safety: Observe chemical safety precautions.

Nothing makes a sailor's life more miserable than water dripping onto his bunk from deck hardware mounting bolts. Worse than an occasional wet pillow is the mildew that inevitably grows in a damp cabin. Moisture from drips allows mildew to bloom in the cabin during periods when the boat is not being used. Come the weekend, you open the hatch and up comes a whiff of that unmistakable musty odor of a closed boat.

All bolt or screw holes through decks or cabin tops must be suspected of allowing water to enter the boat. Cleats generally have four bolt holes—meaning four possible leaks—as do lifeline stanchions and antenna mounts. The number of potential weeping fasteners in the average boat deck can be astounding. A 19-foot Typhoon sloop has more than five dozen holes for bolts or screws. A bigger, more complex boat will have ten or twenty times that many fasteners. Each hole is a possible leak.

Discovering just which fastener is leaking can be frustrating. Thanks to capillary action, water *can* move uphill to make its appearance somewhere totally unrelated to its point of entry. An old-timer's trick for tracing water is to sprinkle ordinary baby powder on wet horizontal surfaces. A light

dusting will do. The powder floats and moves with otherwise imperceptible currents. The source of the leak is "upstream," as indicated by the powder.

Remove the Piece

The only way to cure leaking deck hardware is to lift the offending piece and rebed it with fresh caulking. Loosening bolts requires two people: one works with a wrench on the inside nuts while the other holds a screwdriver in the bolt heads outside. Women and children, because of their smaller size, are usually better suited for the inside work (as long as they're not claustrophobic).

Communication between the inside and outside workers can be a problem. Work out a system of describing bolts so both people have their tools on the same fastener. The four bolts on a cleat might be described as *port forward, port aft, starboard forward*, and *starboard aft*.

Old bedding material must be removed both from the base of the piece of hardware and from the deck or cabin top. Hard chunks of old bedding will prevent new caulking from sealing. Clean everything to "like new" condition. Apply new bedding following the instructions in Chapter 2 (see Bedding Materials," page 17). Observe precautions against creating a "dry joint" when tightening the mounting hardware.

Deck hardware must be reinstalled with all of the backing plates, lock washers, and locking nuts originally used by the factory. This is especially true of cleats, which come under considerable strain. Backing plates spread this strain over the widest possible area; without them, the strain is concentrated in one small area of the deck, which could fail catastrophically. People get hurt when cleats pull off the deck.

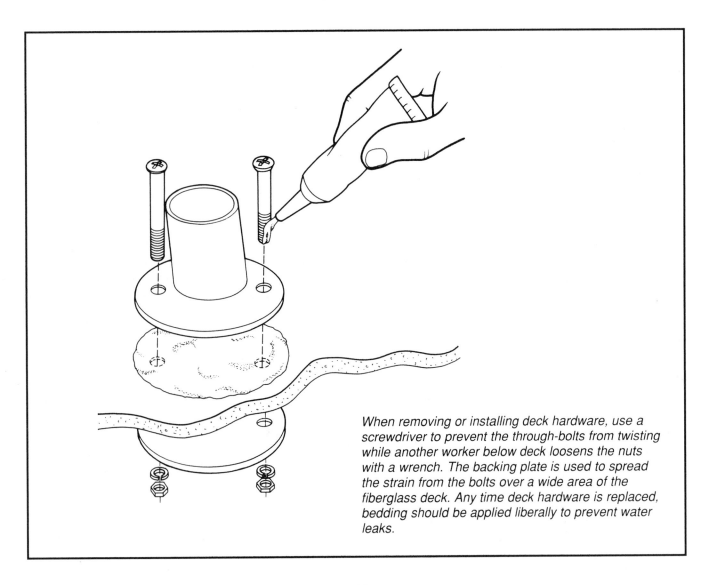

When removing or installing deck hardware, use a screwdriver to prevent the through-bolts from twisting while another worker below deck loosens the nuts with a wrench. The backing plate is used to spread the strain from the bolts over a wide area of the fiberglass deck. Any time deck hardware is replaced, bedding should be applied liberally to prevent water leaks.

CRAZED OR SCRATCHED PLASTIC WINDOWS

Time: Varies with job; usually under one hour.

Materials: Polishing compound, toothpaste, Brasso, carnauba wax, rags.

Tools: Hand buffing pads.

Safety: Observe chemical safety.

Clear plastic glazing materials are used for everything from portholes to venturi windshields. The optical properties of modern clear plastics rival the best glass. Many space-age plastics simply won't shatter, a decided safety advantage. Unfortunately, none of the plastic glazing materials used on boats are as scratch-resistant as glass. Nor are they resistant to damage from harsh cleaning chemicals. Scratches and surface "crazing" are common on plastic glazing.

Crazing

Crazing is the term for spiderweb scratches that appear to cover a large area of a hatch or window. They are often invisible when the sun is directly overhead, but become very apparent in low-angle sunlight. On close inspection, crazing seems to lie on the surface of the plastic, but no scratches or imperfections can be felt with the fingertips.

Crazing can be caused by using the wrong cleaning agents. Many household products labeled as "glass cleaners" contain alcohol, ammonia, or other caustic chemicals that are perfectly safe on glass but can harm plastic materials. They cause a type of "chemical weathering" that leaves the surface damaged in much the same manner as long-term exposure to tropical sunlight.

Chemical damage is insidious. Nothing happens for a few days or weeks after using the wrong cleaner. The window or hatch appears sparkling clean. Then, almost overnight, crazing appears.

Crazing of new plastic can be delayed by cleaning only with fresh water and nothing more. Some crazing will eventually take place due to exposure to ultraviolet light from the sun. Ordinarily, this aging effect is of little structural importance, as long as it remains just on the surface. But hatches that get walked on (foredeck hatches on sailboats, for instance) deserve extra attention to be sure that crazing does not hide actual structural cracks.

Scratches

Scratches are deep damage to the surface of the plastic. Material is removed in the process of creating a scratch, so there is a groove or indentation that can be felt with the fingertips. Scratches show up when oblique light from the sun strikes the side walls of the grooves. Being rough, the side walls refract the light in a random pattern instead of allowing it to pass through without distortion.

Clouding

Clouding is a general "milky" appearance in the plastic. It is often an internal change in the material that cannot be reversed or removed. Older materials became cloudy rather quickly because they were less stable in sunlight. Better ultraviolet protection has all but eliminated this problem from modern plastic glazing. Once true clouding takes place, the only fix is to replace the offending piece.

A form of surface clouding results from using gritty cleaning products. This clouding is not inside the physical composition of the plastic; rather, it is the result of a billion microscopic scratches on the surface so close together that the plastic appears fogged or milky. This sort of clouding is easily prevented by not using gritty cleansers on clear plastic. Even cleaning agents labeled safe for fiberglass may cloud a plastic hatch or window.

Restoring Plastic Glazing

Traditional home restoration for crazing or scratches involves reducing the offending refraction of the side walls of the scratches. This is done in two ways:

Waxing: A quick temporary fix. Small scratches can be filled with wax to reduce light refraction from the side walls of the scratches and make them almost (but not quite) invisible. Carnauba paste wax works best. Liquid waxes do virtually nothing to fill scratches. Wax is a temporary fix that requires renewing at regular intervals.

Buffing: Permanent removal of scratches or crazing is accomplished by buffing them with special, extremely mild abrasives. Extreme caution and the right equipment must be used or serious damage can be done.

Some people have had good results removing scratches with mild abrasive products such as toothpaste, baking soda, and even Brasso metal polish. None of these remedies can be recommended without reservations.

Micro-Resurfacing

Airlines fix the acrylic plastic windows in their planes with buffing materials from Micro-Surface Finishing Products, Inc., of Wilton, Iowa. This company has just introduced consumer kits under the brand name Sand'nShine. These kits contain the same Micro-Mesh polishing materials and chemicals used on airliners.

The Sand'nShine system uses ultrafine "sandpaper" to remove scratches and surface imperfections in acrylics. No ordinary sandpaper, Micro-Mesh materials are cloth-backed, cushioned abrasives with resilient material between the backing and the abrasive. Grits soar far beyond the 1,800 starting grit. Final buffing is done with an 8,000 "grit," so fine that it feels like glove leather.

Start the process by wrapping the 1,800 Micro-Mesh around the foam block supplied in the kit. This is rubbed in a *straight line* over the damaged area. *Never* use a circular motion. Once the scratches have been removed, go to the 2,400 grit and continue working, *but at right angles* to the original motion. This removes the minute scratch pattern left by the 1,800 Micro-Mesh. Then switch

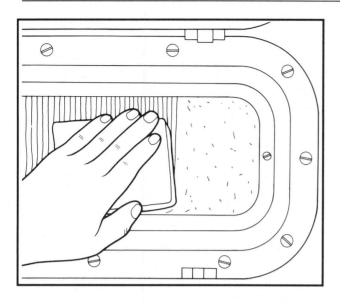

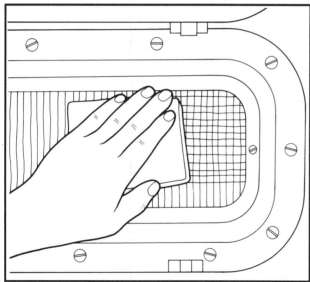

A hard foam-rubber block and special sandpaper are the secrets to one method of restoring acrylic window glazing. Start with 400 grit paper, always working with a straight-line motion (top). Move up through the grits, sanding at a right angle to the previous grit with each change (bottom). Final polishing is done with fine 4,000 or 6,000 grits. Never work in a circular motion, as this will result in swirl marks.

to 3,200 and work in the original direction. This alternate motion continues through 4,000, 6,000, and 8,000 grit materials. The final polish is an anti-static cream.

Replacing Plastic Glazing

In larger cities you'll find commercial plastics houses that stock a wide variety of acrylic and polycarbonate suitable for boat windows and hatches. These companies will cut and drill pieces to order for an additional charge. Take advantage of these services, as cutting plastic is a specialized art. To be sure the plastic house produces an exact replacement piece, give them the old one as a pattern.

Metal hardware should be removed from the old piece before taking it to the plastic company, but leave O-ring seals in place to guide the cutting of the new piece. Be sure to describe exactly what the piece is used for on the boat and any unusual strain it may encounter. This will help the professional select the proper replacement plastic.

POLISHING BRIGHT METALS

Time: Varies with job.

Materials: Metal cleaner, polish, rags.

Tools: None.

Safety: Observe chemical safety; use skin and eye protection.

In Gilbert and Sullivan's comic opera *H.M.S. Pinafore*, the admiral admits he got his job by "polishing the brass of the Queen's Nay-Vee." The song is a spoof on the British navy's penchant for polishing, cleaning, or painting everything on shipboard. Perhaps the military overdoes things like brass polishing, but there's no doubt that sailors have always been proud of their ships. Care of exterior metal is one way to show that pride.

Aluminum

Unprotected aluminum develops a protective tarnish that retards but does not prevent corrosion, especially in salt water. The surface of unprotected aluminum becomes pitted as it slowly deteriorates. Anodizing is the most common way of protecting aluminum, especially for masts and booms of sailboats. In anodizing, the surface of the metal is deliberately corroded under controlled conditions through the use of heavy electrical current. Properly anodized aluminum is highly resistant to tarnishing, but this protection is easily scratched or chafed off.

It is impossible to repair damage to anodizing yourself, so care should be exercised in handling aluminum parts. Aluminum masts and booms should be routinely hosed down with fresh water to remove salt buildup. An annual coat of hard carnauba wax is recommended.

Brass

Brass is an alloy of copper and zinc that does not weather well, especially around salt water, where it turns green and splotchy. Brass can be kept looking "Bristol" by bringing it to a high polish and then coating it with either clear lacquer or plastic spray. Light tarnish is best removed with a wadding polish such as Flitz or Never Dull. Wadding polish works chemically on the surface of the metal to remove tarnish, so there is little chance of scratching. Heavily tarnished or corroded metal will need the stronger approach of liquid metal polish, such as Brasso.

Brass should be avoided below the waterline. Long exposure in salt water can cause a chemical change to the metal known as "de-zincification."

Zinc is removed from brass alloys by this process, leaving behind only the soft copper. There is no repair for de-zincification. The ruined part must be replaced.

Bronze

Bronze is an alloy of copper and tin that has a much higher resistance to corrosion than brass. Although it does not corrode rapidly, bronze will tarnish when exposed to salt water. Over time, this tarnish becomes a dark green patina (verdigris) that protects the metal somewhat. Most owners simply "let nature take its course," as the patina is not unattractive. The only disadvantage is the possibility of dark green stains on the topsides where water runs off porthole spigots and other fittings.

Bronze can be made Bristol with liquid metal polish and elbow grease. Since many bronze items are functional parts of the boat, coating them with lacquer or spray plastic is not practical. Carnauba past wax provides short-lived protection, but frequent repolishing will be needed to maintain bright bronze.

Ordinary (Mild) Steel

Ordinary iron and steel are seldom used as part of modern boat construction except as part of the ground tackle. Anchors, anchor chains, and shackles are all subject to the most common form of metal corrosion: rust. The most practical way of protecting against rust is to dip these items in molten zinc in a process called "galvanizing." The resulting zinc coating protects the underlying steel until it is scratched or worn off.

Steel can be re-galvanized as often as needed. Companies specializing in galvanizing can be found in large cities. Two-part epoxy paints also work well at protecting steel from corrosion but are too soft for use on ground tackle. Paint will wear off during just one night of anchoring in a sandy bottom.

Stainless Steel

The name "stainless steel" refers to a whole range of steel alloys, not to a single specific metal. Most "stainless" used on boats is of the austenitic variety, which is typically nonmagnetic. New rails and other fittings may occasionally exhibit rust stains caused by iron particles embedded in the surface by tools used during the manufacturing process. Rust stains that emerge from the underside of fittings are an indication of a water "sandwich" between the fitting and the deck. Lifting the fitting and rebedding is the fix.

Salt and dirt buildup should always be scrubbed off the metal with soap and plenty of fresh water. Metal polishes will restore the bright appearance, although it is not necessary to purchase special products to care for stainless-steel fittings. Boat polishes such as Star brite do the job as well as most metal-only products and provide some protection to the stainless.

UPGRADING NAVIGATION LIGHT LENSES

Time: Ten minutes.

Materials: New lenses.

Tools: Screwdriver.

Safety: No special requirements.

Navigation lights (running lights) use plastic lenses to focus the light from the bulb and to color the light red or green for sidelights. When new, plastic lenses are good enough to meet stringent Coast Guard standards on visibility and color saturation of navigation lights. After a few years, many plastic lenses begin to show their age.

Colored lenses fail first, losing their deep red or green color, so that even at a modest distance they appear to be ordinary white lights. Over time, ultraviolet light from the sun clouds clear lenses so that they no longer meet minimum visibility standards. Fixing either problem is easy and inexpensive. Replacement lenses for most light fixtures cost less than two dollars at most chandleries.

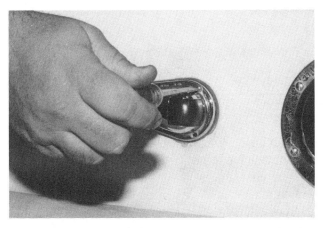

The metal or plastic body of most navigation lights is held in place by small screws that must be removed to service either the bulb or the colored lens.

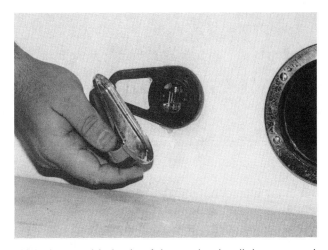

With the outside body of the navigation light removed, the light bulb is easily changed. Remove any corrosion from the contacts before installing a new bulb. The colored lens used on sidelights should be replaced if it has faded or changed color.

Replacing a lens is no more difficult than changing the light bulb. Simply remove the screws holding the body of the light fixture together and the lens should drop out. Disassemble nav lights before buying replacement lenses. Take the old lenses to the store to be sure of getting exact replacements. Drop the new lenses into the fixtures and screw the housing back together. Remember:

RED lens in PORT sidelight.
GREEN lens in STARBOARD sidelight.

Whenever a nav light is disassembled, it's worthwhile to check electrical connections. Corrosion is almost inevitable between the socket and the bulb. Remove it with 220 grit sandpaper rolled into a tube the size of the socket. Rotate the sandpaper in the socket until bright metal shows. Vacuum any sanding dust out of the lamp fixture. Spray the contacts in the socket and the base of the bulb with a moisture-displacing lubricant such as Boeshield T-9, WD-40, or CRC. Replace bulbs every year, even if they are still working, to prevent an unexpected dead lamp later in the season. Keep these old bulbs as spares in a properly marked container.

PORTHOLE AND WINDOW LEAKS

Time: Two and a half hours per porthole.

Materials: Polysulfide caulk, solvent, rags.

Tools: Putty knife, screwdriver, wrench, wood wedges, heat gun.

Safety: Care when using putty knife; hand and eye protection from solvent and caulk; electric tool safety.

A boat would be nothing but a seagoing cave without the light and air from windows and portholes. Unfortunately, any opening that lets light or air into the cabin is also a potential pathway for water. Everyone leaves a porthole open during a thunderstorm at some time during their lives, but that's just an inconvenient mess. Problem leaks are those that come through the joints between the ports, or window frames and the superstructure, or hull topsides. Caulking is the only prevention against leaks here. Sooner or later, the original caulking installed by the factory hardens and cracks. Water follows these cracks into the boat, where it drip, drip, drip, drips onto the captain's head while he tries to sleep.

Easy-Fix Failure

There's a great temptation to buy a tube of silicone sealer and goop up the outside of the port. Theoretically, this solution should work, but it never does. The leaks still drip despite the smeared silicone, which invariably catches dirt and turns black. Forget the easy-fix approach. The only way to repair leaks permanently is to open the offending joints and renew the caulking.

Portholes

The frame of the typical metal porthole is installed on the inside of the boat. It has a hinge that allows the glass to open (known as a portlight) and dogs to keep the glass closed in a seaway. Around the opening in the frame is a metal rim, called the spigot. This rim goes through the hole in the cabin wall and extends ½ to ¾ of an inch on the outside. A trim ring is installed around the spigot on the outside to give the porthole a finished appearance. Bolts through the trim ring, fiberglass, and frame hold everything together. Leaks will be found under the trim ring in the caulking between the cabin cutout and the spigot.

Rebedding a porthole involves removing the bolts and lifting the trim ring. Unless the old caulk is really dead, the trim ring won't pop off very easily. A bit of work will be needed to break the grip of the old sealant. Sliding a putty knife between the trim ring and the fiberglass should cut the old caulking. Metallic black marks left by the putty knife can be removed with rubbing compound. Work carefully to avoid scratching the gel coat.

Small wedges cut from scrap wood can also be used to force metal trim rings away from the hull. Create an opening between the hull and ring with a putty knife; then gently drive a wedge. Don't try to lift the ring in just one spot. Work all the way around the ring with wedges to avoid bending the metal. It may take a dozen or more wedges to lift the whole ring. An hour isn't too long to spend doing this part of the job correctly. Some types of caulking respond well to heat from a heat gun. In a pinch, even a hair-dryer may help soften old caulking.

A real problem crops up if polyurethane sealer/adhesive was used to bed the trim ring. In this case, the ring will be so stuck to the boat that the fiberglass may pull apart before the sealer breaks loose. The only way to lift a trim ring that's been glued to the boat is to cut the adhesive. Try sharpening the front edge of a rigid putty knife. Put a knife-sharp edge on it with a grinding wheel. Drive that sharp edge between the trim ring and the fiberglass with light taps of a hammer. Pull it out, move it a blade's width and drive it in again. Expect to spend a couple of hours repeating this operation until the seal around the trim ring has been cut. Some damage to the fiberglass beneath the trim ring always occurs during this laborious process.

The old caulking should hold the porthole frame in place in the cabin wall while the trim ring is lifted. If not, duct tape makes a great "third hand." Tape the frame in position from the inside. Little or no sticky tape residue will remain if the tape is peeled off within a few hours. Any remaining goo can be cleaned off with mineral spirits.

Pull out all loose old caulking from the gap between the port frame and the cabin. An electrician's screwdriver is a good tool for this job. Clean any old caulking off the trim ring. Using a caulking gun, squirt new polysulfide caulking into the gap between spigot and cabin side. Then put a bead around the back side of the trim ring. (Portholes eat up a lot of caulking.) Don't worry about trying to produce a neat bead of caulking because the trim ring will be squished down on top of it.

Installing the trim ring and tightening the bolts

should squeeze caulking out all around the spigot and the ring. Scrape up the excess with a putty knife and wipe it onto a small piece of cardboard. Excess caulking can be used before it sets up to bed another porthole or some other piece of hardware.

Fixed (Nonopening) Windows

There are so many types of window frames that it is impossible to give instructions on fixing all of them. Frames that use a "live" rubber gasket can be fixed only by obtaining a replacement gasket. Plastic frames require extreme care when lifting the outer trim ring to avoid breakage. Some windows will literally fall out of the boat when the trim ring is lifted, while other designs stay comfortably in place while being caulked. The only sure advice is to study the individual window carefully before taking things apart. Most of all, never force plastic!

PRO TIP

Silicone caulking is not the best choice for portholes or windows. It will seal well at first, but it can peel loose inside the joint and allow water to enter. Polysulfide caulks don't develop this problem and are a much better choice. Avoid polyurethane adhesive/sealants, as they make future repairs almost impossible.

OILING TEAK TRIM

Time: Varies with job.

Materials: Teak cleaner, mild soap, teak oil, solvent, disposable brush, sandpaper, rags.

Tools: Soft nylon brush, Scotch-Brite pad, bucket, hose with nozzle, electric palm sander, goggles, rubber gloves.

Safety: Hand and eye protection from harsh cleaners and solvents; electric tool safety. Rags used with teak oil pose serious fire danger due to spontaneous combustion.

Nothing does more to give a boat that "yacht" look than the warm glow of oiled teak. And nothing frustrates boat owners more than trying to keep that warm glow in the exterior teak trim of their boats. On some far-off South Sea island where they've never even heard of air pollution, teak trim would weather to a glorious silver-gray. Unfortunately, most boats live where airborne dirt and chemicals are facts of life. In the industrialized world, exterior teak quickly turns black and lifeless without proper protection and regular cleaning.

Cleaning Exterior Teak

Fresh-sanded teak ranges in color from golden to dark brown. This is the look that all teak maintenance intends to achieve. If the teak is new from the factory, it's usually possible to skip the cleaning stage. But wood that has been exposed to the atmosphere for even a few weeks will need at least a soap-and-water washdown.

Airborne dirt and the weathering of the natural oil in the wood cause teak to turn black and ugly. Teak cleaners remove the buildup of old dirty oils—that's good. What's bad about chemical cleaners is that they also remove the soft pithy wood fibers that lie between ribbons of harder growth wood. As a rule of thumb, the stronger the cleaner, the more pith it removes. The end result of using chemical cleaners is exaggerated grain structure.

Removal of soft wood fibers is accelerated by the use of stiff scrub brushes. Because teak suffers from this problem, there are two general rules to follow in teak maintenance:

1. Use the mildest cleaner possible. Start with mild soap and water. If that doesn't work, move to a one-part proprietary teak cleaner. Save

Specially made soft-bristled brushes designed to be kind to wet teak wood should be used to scrub teak. Stiff bristles will remove the softer portions of the grain, leaving a rough surface. If a soft brush is not available, try a nylon pot scrubber. Be sure to wear protective gloves and goggles when working with harsh teak-cleaning chemicals.

those two-part cleaners for industrial-strength dirt.

2. Never use a stiff-bristle scrub brush. Soft-bristle nylon brushes are okay, but a better bet are the pads sold in grocery stores as pot scrubbers. These pads clean the surface much like fine sandpaper, leaving the pithy wood intact.

Both one- and two-part teak cleaners are relatively harsh on human skin. They dry out the natural oils, causing the skin to crack and bleed. Rubber gloves are essential for hand protection. These chemicals are also hard on the eyes. Since splashing is an inevitable part of scrubbing, protective goggles are suggested. As with all chemical products, *read and follow the instructions on the package.* Teak cleaners must be kept out of the hands of small children; and pets should be kept away from areas where teak cleaning products are in use.

All chemical residue must be rinsed out of the wood after cleaning. This is best with fresh water from a dockside hose. High pressure isn't necessary, just a thorough drenching of the cleaned wood. Continue rinsing for several minutes after the last of the suds or dirt from the cleaner comes out of the wood. If in doubt, rinse again. Let the wood dry for several hours in the hot noonday sun.

Sanding Clean Teak

First of all, remember this: Never sand wet wood.

Cleaning teak with chemicals always raises some grain. Light hand sanding with 80 grit paper should restore the smooth surface unless there has been severe weathering. In that case, an electric palm sander with 80 grit paper should do the job. Sand only enough to restore a reasonably smooth surface. Some grain ridges should be considered normal in exterior teak. Excessive sanding will achieve a glass-smooth surface, but after a few seasons the trim will have been sanded off the boat!

Believe it or not, 80 grit paper is "finish sanding" on teak. True, the wood will get smoother by going up the grits to 100, 150, and even 320. But, there is a negative side effect to getting teak exceptionally smooth. It actually burnishes the surface and effectively "case hardens" it against the penetration of teak oil and other protective finishes. The result is that an oil finish on teak sanded beyond 80 grit does not last as long as it would have if the teak had been left a tad rougher.

Choosing and Applying Teak Oil

Now hear this: When it comes to choosing teak oil, you'll get no help from me—no direct suggestions on which product to use. Over the years I've tried just about all of the major brands and found that most work as claimed. The big differences come in longevity of the finish. Discussions with other boat owners and repairmen indicate that some brands work better in one part of the country than another. The amount of direct sunlight and air pollution are probably factors in the geographic variations. The best advice is to check around the marinas near you to see which boats display the teak look you desire. Talk to the owners of those boats for recommendations.

A wide variety of products are sold under the generic description "teak oil." Some are true oils, but many are modern chemical concoctions with nary a drop of oil. Application of these teak products can be done with a brush or a rag. Some manufacturers specify rag application in the belief that hand pressure helps push the product into the wood fibers. Another company says that a disposable foam brush is the best applicator. Both techniques can be used to advantage. Foam brushes are excellent for long, broad stretches of wood. Rags make application easier on curved or irregular surfaces such as handrails.

One coat of any teak product won't last an August afternoon. Two, three, or more coats are always needed. Some products, like Flood's Deks Olje, say to continue applying until no more can be absorbed by the wood. This can mean six, eight, or even ten coats. *Read and follow the manufacturer's instructions.* It's a lot easier to apply enough coats the first time than to do the whole job over again every couple of weeks.

Teak Oil Problems

Factory people say that applying an oil finish on water-damp wood is a sure ticket to disaster. One oil manufacturer blames residual moisture for the growth of black mold beneath the coating provided by his product. This mold lives on the natural oils in the teak. So make sure the wood is absolutely dry before applying the finish. A couple of hours of hot tropical sun will probably do it, but the same amount of cool New England sun might not be enough drying.

Some professional boat detailers insist on removing as much of the natural oil from the teak as possible prior to applying any finish. They do this with acetone rubdowns, constantly turning the rag to avoid spreading the natural wood oils trapped in the cloth. The acetone is then allowed to "flash off" ("dry") for twenty minutes before application of finish coats begins.

If at all possible, avoid applying teak oils or other finish products in direct sunlight or during the hottest part of the day. In the morning, this limits you to those hours after the dew has dried and before approximately 11:00 A.M. Afternoon work should not begin before 3:00 P.M. and must be completed at least an hour before the dew is expected to settle.

Some oil or other finish product is always spilled on the deck. This usually wipes up with a dry rag. The residue from natural oil products can be removed with mineral spirits. Once dry, teak oil is extremely difficult to remove without resorting to fiberglass-safe paint remover. Some non-oil products use unexpected solvents. Teak Guard, for instance, recommends using lacquer thinner as a cleaning agent.

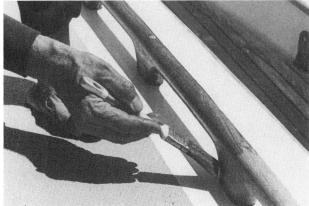

Teak oil may be applied with either a rag or a brush. This worker is using a high-quality bristle brush to control the flow of oil onto a cabin handrail. Brushing avoids messy cleanup that sometimes results from using a rag. However, some teak oil manufacturers suggest application with a rag as a way of achieving deeper penetration. Oiled wood is noticeably darker and has more pronounced grain than dry wood.

Mid-Season Touchup

Different teak finishes have different lifespans, all of them limited. Tropical sun can limit some brands to less than a week of life while others may last six weeks under the same conditions. Eventually, however, all oils or other finishes must be renewed. The exact procedure varies from product to product. *Read and follow the manufacturer's instructions regarding touchup procedures.* As a general rule, the wood must be washed with mild soap to remove surface dirt and rinsed with fresh water. The wood is then allowed to dry before top coats of new finish are applied.

FIRE SAFETY WARNING

Rags soaked in teak oils containing linseed oil pose a danger of spontaneous combustion. Never ball them up in a waste basket. Wash them immediately in hot soap and water, then spread them out to air dry. You can also burn oil-saturated rags in an approved incinerator. In any case, never store oil-soaked rags aboard the boat, in the trunk of a car, or inside a building.

REPLACING A BILGE VENT COWL

Time: Forty-five minutes; longer if vent hose must be replaced.

Materials: New cowl, replacement hose, oval head stainless-steel self-tapping screws, stainless-steel 4-inch hose clamp, polysulfide caulk, solvent, rags.

Tools: Screwdriver, putty knife, wire cutters, sharp knife.

Safety: Chemical safety with solvent; it is critical to vent explosive fumes from bilge and engine compartment.

Coast Guard regulations require ventilation of the bilge and engine compartment to prevent explosions. Ventilators must be installed on power-boats before they are sold, so it is seldom necessary to retrofit them to existing boats. More common is the need to replace the metal or plastic cowl on deck that scoops up fresh air. Even the best of these can be damaged by a misplaced foot or a dropped anchor.

The typical vent is a clamshell affair held to the deck by screws. It has a short neck that extends below deck level, where it connects to 3-inch plastic vent hose. Some vents are designed for 4-inch hose, but these are rare. Cowls are available in soft plastic, chromed Zamak, and stainless steel. Surprisingly, soft plastic vents often outlast metal when it comes to taking abuse. They are made of the same flexible white material as boat fenders, so they can take hard knocks without complaint.

Removing Old Vents

Most vents are secured to the deck by three self-tapping screws. A seal of caulk may hold the old vent down after the screws are removed. Use a stiff-blade putty knife to break this seal. Lift the old vent carefully, as the vent hose will be attached with less than 6 inches of slack. Old vent hose is notoriously brittle and often the entire section must be replaced once it starts cracking.

Two methods are used for securing the hose to the neck of the vent. The simplest is a hose clamp. Loosen the clamp screw and the hose should slide off the neck. The other method of attachment involves lugs that catch on the reinforcing wire of the vent hose. Try "unscrewing" this type of vent from the hose. If that doesn't work, the only solution is force. Pulling the old vent out usually damages the hose, so use force only as a last resort.

Check the vent hose for cuts, tears, or damage down inside the gunwale. A flashlight can illuminate down to the first bend. Avoid replacing this hose if possible, as it is a frustrating job at best. However, torn or broken vent hoses have contributed to engine compartment fires and explosions on gasoline-powered boats. It is vital that vent hoses be undamaged if they are going to ventilate explosive fumes out of the bilge.

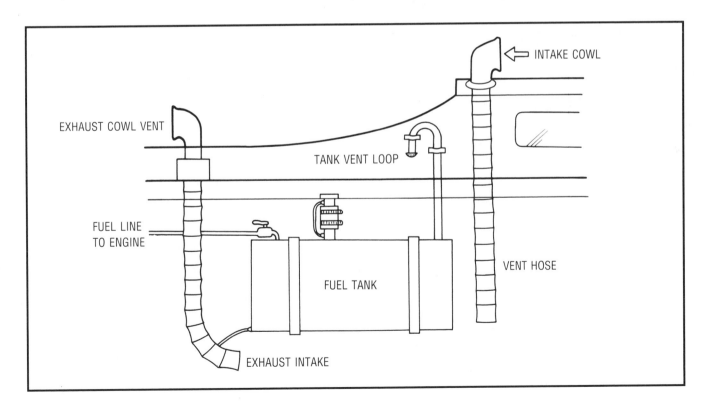

There is no easy way to snake new vent hose into most old boats. Vent hoses are built into the boat before the deck and internal furniture are installed. Repairmen can spend hours concocting "Rube Goldberg" devices to pull new hose through the narrow, twisting path from deck to bilge. It's often easier to run new hose on the surface and build a protective cover around it. Make the cover of teak or mahogany to match the boat.

Installing the new ventilator is a matter of attaching the vent hose and screwing the unit to the deck with a bit of new caulking. Old screw holes won't match the new fitting unless it's an exact replacement. Fill the old holes with polyester putty and gel coat if they show (see the discussion on gouges in Chapter 3, page 67). A dab of polysulfide caulk in the old holes will waterproof them if they do not show. Polysulfide caulk should also be used to seal the new vent to the deck. This is not a place for polyurethane adhesive/sealant because cowl vents need to be replaced from time to time. Polyurethane would make the vent a permanent fixture.

REPAIRING BROKEN WINDSHIELD WIPERS

Time: Two minutes for the blade; thirty minutes for motor replacement.

Materials: New blade, new motor.

Tools: Screwdriver, wrench, pliers.

Safety: Exercise caution against falling when working on upper decks.

Wiper Blade Replacement

Rubber windshield wiper blades are subject to ozone and ultraviolet light deterioration. Replacement is necessary every year to continue streak-free operation. New blades are available in a variety of lengths, but most boat stores stock only one or two popular lengths. Longer blades are available on special order.

Replacing a wiper blade is one of the easiest jobs on a boat. Pull the spring-loaded wiper arm gently away from the windshield. The old blade is unhooked from the arm and the new one hooked into place. A simple hook is used on older-style blades. Newer designs use a "push-click" attachment similar to automobiles. Allow the blade to snap back against the glass and the job's done.

Wiper Motor Replacement

Marine windshield-wiper motors seldom last forever. Salt water eventually works its way down the actuating shaft and into the motor itself. Corrosion takes its toll and the wiper stops working. Repairing a corroded or broken motor is seldom possible. Replacement is the only practical fix.

Cheaply made replacement motors abound in the marine aftermarket. They are hard to tell from the higher-quality motors. Since wiper motor longevity depends on the basic quality of the machine, spend a few bucks more and get a better motor. Marine wiper motors haven't changed substantially in decades, so it should be possible to find almost an exact replacement. Pay particular attention to shaft diameter. Motors are available with ⅝-, ½-, and ⅜-inch shafts.

Disconnect only one wire at a time from the old motor. Label the wire with a masking tape flag before disconnecting the next wire. This will avoid confusion when connecting the new motor. There should be three wires: a "hot" wire; one from the switch; and a ground wire. Mark each wire with the terminal identification stamped on the wiper motor body. The following table shows the typical color code for the wires and corresponding terminal identifications:

Once the wires are marked, the old motor can be removed. Loosen the clamping screw on the wiper arm and remove the arm from the outside shaft. This exposes a large nut on the shaft that holds the motor in place. Loosen this nut and pull off the metal grommet and rubber washer beneath it. Pull the motor unit backwards out of the windshield frame.

Installation of the new unit is pretty much the reverse of removing the old one. The only special consideration is to adjust the projection of the

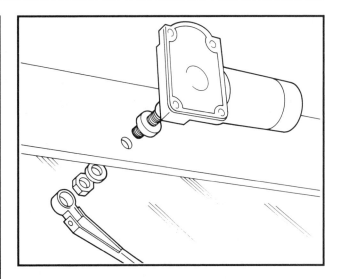

Replacing a windshield wiper motor is a simple task. Remove and mark the electrical wires. Then remove the wiper arm and loosen the retaining nut. Pull the motor stud back through the windshield. Install a new motor by reversing these steps. Be sure to include the rubber compression washers, which prevent leaks.

shaft through the windshield frame. A nut on the portion of the shaft inside the frame does the adjusting. The new motor should come with two metal grommets and two rubber washers. One washer-and-grommet set goes inside and the other goes on the outside of the frame. The metal grommet always goes against the nut, while the rubber washer is always in contact with the windshield frame to insure a watertight fit.

Second Wiper Installation

Most boats come with only one wiper on the windshield—directly in front of the helmsman. Installing

WINDSHIELD-WIPER CONNECTIONS

Purpose	Wire Color	Terminal Identification
Power from Control Switch	Red	"S" or "ON"
Unswitched Power from Positive (+) Bus	Blue	"+" or "OFF"
Ground Wire (−)	Black	"GND"

Table 4.1

a second wiper to improve vision through the entire windshield is not difficult. The new wiper can be installed either at the top of the windshield (through the frame), or at the bottom (through the deck). Top mounting is common on opening windshield vents. Deck mounting can be used only on windshields that do not open. A special angle bracket is needed for through-deck installations.

Installation starts by drilling a hole the correct size for the wiper motor shaft. This hole is located on the centerline of the area to be wiped. The motor is then mounted as described above. Wires should be run carefully to keep them from being pinched when the windshield is opened or closed. Follow the color code in Table 4.1.

Electrical connections may be made to the existing wiper switch, but this is not the best practice. Boats often take spray on only one side. If both motors are wired to the same switch, one will be wiping dry glass while the other is lubricated by water from the spray. The dry wiper will not only wear out faster, but may also create scratches (especially on plastic glazing). It's usually best to give each wiper its own switch to prevent this situation.

The Parking Circuit

The circuit that "parks" the wiper blade at one side of the windshield often creates confusion. The parking circuit has a switch inside the motor that is automatically turned on when the wiper arm is anywhere in its wiping arc. This keeps power coming to the motor even when the switch on the control console is turned off. The motor keeps running until the wiper arm reaches one end of its travel, where the parking switch automatically cuts off power. Naturally, the wiper arm stops moving in its "parked" position at one end of its travel.

Wiring the parking circuit is not necessary. Power can be fed from the control console switch directly to the "S" (or "ON") terminal of the wiper motor. The "+" (or "OFF") terminal can be left disconnected. With a proper ground wire attached, the wiper motor will run as long as the console switch is on. Turning the switch off will cause the wiper arm to stop moving wherever it is located on the windshield. Parking the blade at one end of its travel must be done "manually" by turning the switch off at the exact right instant.

CHAPTER 5

THE INTERIOR

Working on the outside of a boat is easy. It's pretty much all done standing up, except for renewing the antifouling. Inside, however, things change. Space is confined and jobs often require twisting into a body pretzel just to reach the last nut or at-tach the final connection. On the good side, work can be done in the cabin even when the boat is in winter storage. In fact, many of the following projects are excellent over-the-winter improvements.

INSTALLING BUNK LIGHTS

Time: About one hour per light.

Materials: Bunk light fixture, wire, crimp connectors, screws, trim molding, solder, heat-shrinkable tubing, rosin core solder.

Tools: Drill motor, drill bits, soldering iron, screwdriver, wire cutters, wire stripper, fish wire.

Safety: Electric tool safety; fire safety if soldering iron is used.

Each bunk should have a private light. In addition to being useful for reading, it comes in handy when the sleeper needs to get up in the middle of the night to use the head. A small light is far less likely to wake up other sleepers than the overhead cabin dome light. The exact choice of a light fixture is determined by personal taste and consideration of the space available, but small fixtures are generally better than big, powerful ones in this application.

There are two interrelated problems to installing bunk lights. The first is finding a 12-volt power source, and the second is hiding the wires. As a general rule, it's best to tap into the boat's main lighting circuit for power. This prevents draining the battery if a bunk light is accidentally left on. Flipping the cabin light switch off at the main switch panel will douse the bunk lights as well.

Avoid tapping into a circuit normally left "off" when the boat is docked or at anchor. Tapping the navigation light circuit, for example, would result in the bunk lights being useless except when the boat is under way at night.

Hiding the Wires

Hiding electrical wires is a test of creativity. It was easy back at the factory because the wiring was done before the deck was installed. Everything was accessible. Once the deck was installed, the wires became hidden inside fiberglass liners and molded-in furniture. Installing new light fixtures often requires the surface mounting of wires on bulkheads or headliners. Surface wiring is never pretty and can be downright ugly. The goal is to hide wiring or make it unobtrusive when it can't be hidden.

Always run the wiring before installing the light fixture. Many times, the location selected for the light is not possible because of wiring problems.

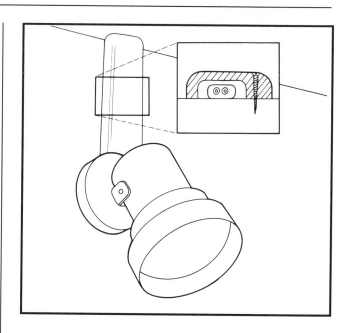

This bunk light is an all-metal fixture that can be swiveled to beam light where desired. Electrical wiring runs on the surface of the bulkhead to the cabin headliner. A wooden wire molding can be used to hide the wires. Power for the light comes from the main cabin lighting circuit. Low-voltage wires are hidden under liners (inset).

Often, wiring must be run behind molded fiberglass interior liners. An electrician's fish tape can be a real help, but the clearance may be too small for a conventional tape. A length of stainless-steel seizing wire makes an excellent substitute fish tape in confined quarters. Seizing wire is commonly used aboard sailboats for holding shrouds in the tips of spreaders or for keeping anchor shackle pins from unscrewing. It is small enough in diameter to get through tight spots yet is strong enough to be pushed around bends.

Use Table 2.7, "Noncritical Applications," in Chapter 2, page 61, to select the proper size electrical wire for 12 volts. Bunk lights draw very little current, so using the smallest acceptable gauge wire will make fishing behind interior liners a lot easier. Two-conductor wire also makes the job easier, since the fishing process has to be done only once instead of twice as it would if individual wires were used. A continuous run of wire is always preferable to a feed line with several splices.

Commercial surface-mount wiring conduit is available in white, brown, and ivory from home improvement stores. This conduit is usually too large for use on a boat, though it may be the right solution in some situations. It can be relatively unobtrusive when installed on white or off-white backgrounds. Brown molding works on dark woods such as mahogany, but is a poor match for teak interiors.

Crimp-on butt connectors make tapping into the 12-volt power source relatively easy. Sometimes, though, it may be desirable to connect into the middle of a long length of wire. In these cases, strip about an inch of insulation from the feed wire without cutting it. Wrap the end of the bunk light wire around the exposed power-source wire and solder this joint. Soldered connections must be protected with high-quality electrical tape or heat-shrinkable tubing. Rosin core solder intended for work on electronics makes the cleanest joints. *Never* use soldering paste and solder intended for joining copper plumbing.

Bunk light fixtures should always have built-in switches, so that each sleeper controls his or her own light. Most bunk lights draw so little current that several can be added to a single circuit without overtaxing the circuit breaker or fuse. If current draw is expected to be a problem, it pays to divide the lighting load over two or more fuses or breakers.

HOMEMADE TEAK WIRE MOLDINGS

Wires that have to run on the surface can be hidden behind homemade teak moldings. Start with a 1-inch plank dressed to the standard $\frac{7}{8}$-inch thickness. Using a table saw with a fence, make a saw kerf halfway through the plank about $\frac{1}{4}$ inch from one edge. Move the fence outward the width of a saw kerf and make a second cut. The result should be a channel two saw kerfs wide in the plank. Reset the saw depth to slice off a $\frac{7}{8}$-inch-wide strip. This strip will contain the two-kerf-wide wire channel, but the channel won't be in the center. Instead, it will be offset so that screws can be installed in the thick edge of the molding. Round the corners with sandpaper and finish the wood to match the boat's interior.

INSTALLING CABIN CARPETING

Time: Four hours per cabin.

Materials: Carpet, carpet cement, double-stick tape, staples, brown kraft paper, masking tape.

Tools: Large shears, carpet knife, staple gun, measuring tape, pencil, wallpaper scraper.

Safety: Customary care with sharp tools. Fire safety, as some carpet cements are extremely flammable.

Wall-to-wall carpeting has become as commonplace at sea as it is in homes ashore. Boat builders like carpet because it hides a multitude of construction sins. Buyers enjoy the feel of carpet beneath their feet on chilly mornings. Unfortunately, a boat is not the best environment for carpeting since dirt, salt crystals, and moisture gang up to end its life prematurely. Replacing carpet is usually the first major interior renovation in a boat's life. It's normal for new carpet to be needed long before the rest of the interior begins to show any serious wear.

Choosing New Carpet

A boat cabin is *never* really dry. Compared to the average home, it's downright dank. Ordinary house carpeting, with natural fiber (jute) backing, is not suited for life afloat. The moist atmosphere quickly causes jute to deteriorate. Boat carpet should be constructed entirely of man-made materials. Indoor-outdoor carpeting is obviously the best choice for durability, but it leaves much to be desired for looks. A good grade of nylon or Dacron

carpet should combine a better appearance with reasonable lifespan. Look for carpet treated with one of the patented stain repellents.

Removing Old Carpet

Extreme care should be used in removing the old carpet, for it makes an excellent pattern for cutting the new. Most builders either staple or glue carpet to plywood subdecking. Many do both—ugh! Start removal in the squarest corner of the cabin (or the corner with the fewest complicated jogs or cutbacks). Carefully peel up the corner, working both directions along the perimeter. This job starts hard, but gets easier as more carpet is lifted off the deck.

Staples or tacks holding the carpet will usually pull out of the wooden subdeck as long as the edge of the carpet is straight. Pulling a curved or jogged section will cause the backing of the carpet to rip while the staples remain unmoved. In these cases, each staple must be lifted individually using a pair of pliers or a screwdriver. Glue can be "cut" loose by driving the blade of a wide putty knife between the subdeck and the carpet backing.

Take the old carpet out of the cabin and carefully clean up the mess that remains. Use pliers to remove broken staples. Beware of broken staples sticking out of the wood when working on hands and knees. Vacuum up the inevitable dust and dirt.

Cutting the Rug

If the old rug came up in one piece, it can be used as a pattern for the new one. Unroll the new carpet *upside down* on a clean, flat floor. Then lay the old carpet—*also upside down*—on top of the new. Using a soft pencil, mark the outline of the old carpet on the backing of the new. Cut along this mark, using either large carpet shears or a sharp knife.

Many times the old carpet adheres so tightly to the deck that removing it requires complete destruction. In this case, a paper pattern is needed. To make one, tape pieces of kraft paper (that brown paper used to wrap packages) together on the deck. Trim the paper until it fits into all of the various curves and jogs around the cabin. Before lifting the pattern, be sure to mark the word TOP in big letters on the side of the paper facing up.

Unroll the new carpet *upside down* on a clean, flat floor. Turn the paper pattern over and place it on top of the new carpet. The side of the pattern marked TOP should be down so that the writing does not show. Use several pieces of tape to hold the pattern in position during the marking process. Paper has a tendency to slide on carpet backing. Mark the backing with a soft pencil and cut along the line using carpet shears or a sharp knife.

Installing New Carpet

Roll up the cut carpet with the top (the nap side) to the inside of the roll. (The backing should be on the outside.) Take the roll aboard and align it at the appropriate end of the cabin. Slowly unroll the carpet, being sure that it remains aligned with cabin walls along both sides. Check for fit around doors and under cabinets after rubbing out any "bubbles."

If the fit is acceptable and the new carpet lies tight to the deck, it can be fastened down with rustproof staples or tacks. Staples hide well in loose-nap carpets. An electric or air-powered staple gun makes the job a lot easier. Hand-powered guns do not have enough power to fully set the staples. If a staple does not penetrate completely, a few taps with a hammer should finish the job. Appropriate Monel (stainless-steel) staples are expensive and may be difficult to find. Copper tacks are widely available, but take longer to install than staples.

Nonflammable floor-covering cement can also be used to hold the new carpet in place. After checking the fit of the new carpet, fold back half of it, exposing half of the wood deck. Trowel the cement onto the deck, following the instructions on the can. Unfold the carpet and carefully smooth it onto the adhesive, making sure to press out any "bubbles" or wrinkles.

Now fold back the nonglued section of carpet and repeat the above procedure to complete the installation.

MILDEW PREVENTION AND REMOVAL

Time: Varies with job.

Materials: Ventilator plates, antimildew chemical packets, ordinary mothballs, household chlorine bleach, liquid laundry detergent, commercial mildew removers, clean hot water.

Tools: Bucket, rags.

Safety: Skin and eye protection. Always read and follow instructions when using harsh chemical cleaners.

Mildew damages almost everything and may actually destroy some fabrics. It is also closely related to dreaded dry rot in wooden boats. Prevention is the best way to avoid problems, although that is often easier said than done. Good air circulation is the primary defense against mildew. (See the section on "Improving Cabin Ventilation," page 129.)

Never put anything away wet. This admonition applies equally to foul-weather gear and nylon rope anchor rodes. Neither will be damaged by mildew, but dampness from them can be a major factor in the growth of mildew bacteria elsewhere. Dampness created by wet nylon rope may trigger mildew growth on the mattress in the owner's stateroom.

Avoid using cleaners or polishes on interior fabrics or bulkheads that leave any sort of organic chemical films behind. Such films often provide just enough food for a "bloom" of mildew. For example, Liquid Gold polish works like magic around the house; but at sea, use of this product has been linked to mildew growth.

Fabric items such as clothing, towels, or bedding should not be stored in plastic bags. These bags tend to trap moisture inside, creating a perfect mini-environment for mildew. Clothes that have been starched should also be left ashore. The starch in the material is a gourmet lunch for mildew.

Chemical Prevention

Mildew on cabin bulkheads or built-in seat cushions can be prevented through the use of chemical packets such as Mil-Du-Gas. The crystals inside the packet change into a mildew-killing gas that permeates the entire area. If the smell isn't objectionable, somewhat the same effect can be obtained by using ordinary paradichlorobenzene mothballs (the ones your mother used to protect winter garments). Chemicals are an excellent way of obtaining mildew protection during winter layup.

Removing Mildew Stains

Mildew stains can be difficult or impossible to remove. And the damage many of the chemicals used to remove these stains can do can be even worse than the original mildew. The first step in removing stains is to brush and vacuum the discolored area. Much of the mildew should come off the fabric in this way. A metal suede brush can be most helpful. Use caution to avoid snagging the fabric.

Work slowly and carefully in any attempts to remove stains with chemicals or soap. Start with mild soap and water, moving upward in chemical harshness only when your less damaging efforts don't work. Look for fabric care tags on upholstered items. These give a wealth of information about what cleaning techniques to use and which ones to avoid. Finally, be prepared to live with the evidence of a major mildew attack since—at the risk of repetition—the stains are difficult or impossible to remove.

Fabric Care Code

Under U.S. law, upholstered furniture manufactured after 1970 is supposed to carry a fabric care tag. Through a code, this tag indicates which types of stain removal are safe for the fabrics involved. Here's the code:

Furniture Fabric Spot Removal Code

X: Do not use liquid or foam cleaning agents. Remove soil only by brushing or vacuuming.

W: Water and water-based cleaning agents can safely be used on this fabric. Most foam cleaning agents are water-based, but check label on cleaner.

S: Use NO water on this fabric. Dry clean only.

WS: Use either water-based cleaning agents or dry clean.

If the label allows, a solution of liquid laundry detergent and water can be scrubbed into the fabric to remove much of the stain. Commercial foam cleaners sold for automotive application may also work well. Scrub carefully to avoid over-wetting the underlying padding. Rinse well with fresh water using a damp sponge or rag. If possible, dry in direct sunlight. (The ultraviolet content of sunlight is a great mildew killer.)

Vinyl headliners and folding tops are subject to mildew stains that do not wash away with ordinary soap and water. Star brite makes an excellent spray for the purpose. Nearly as effective is a homemade solution of mild detergent and ordinary household chlorine bleach. Sponge this mixture gently over the surface. Avoid splashing on non-colorfast fabrics, such as blue jeans. Let the cleaner do the work of removing the dark mildew stain. Rinse with plenty of fresh water. Be sure to wear rubber gloves and eye protection and have plenty of ventilation when using chemicals to remove mildew stains.

SPECIAL SAFETY WARNING

Never mix chlorine bleach with ammonia or any cleaning product containing ammonia. The combination of chlorine and ammonia produces a gas that may be toxic.

VARNISHING INTERIOR WOOD

Time: Varies with job.

Materials: Varnish, stain, thinner, sandpaper, dewaxing solvent, tack rag, clean rags.

Tools: Electric sander, sanding pad, shop vacuum, natural bristle brush.

Safety: Electric tool and chemical safety.

Refinishing interior varnished wood is much the same as with exterior wood. The same steps of sanding, staining, and varnishing apply. Since these steps are fully detailed in Chapter 2, there is no need to repeat them here. However, there is one problem encountered on interior wood that is seldom seen outside: furniture polish. It's not unusual to find more wax on the wood than varnish. Old furniture polish must be completely removed. Otherwise, wax on the surface will prevent the new coats of varnish from adhering.

Commercial dewaxing solvents available through paint stores work well. Ordinary mineral spirits is a good second choice. Use plenty of solvent on a plain white paper towel. Keep rotating the paper towel to expose fresh cloth to the wood. The wax and oils will be trapped in the paper. If it is not rotated, old gunk will be redeposited on the wood. Let the solvent completely flash off before dewaxing a second time with fresh solvent and clean paper towels. A third dewaxing may be necessary in severe cases.

Careful Preparation

Care must be exercised not to make a mess of the cabin. Sanding dust, which can be brushed aside on the exterior, becomes a cleanup nightmare inside. A good vacuum is essential to a "clean as you go" policy. Drop cloths should cover virtually everything that is not going to be varnished. Spills and splashes have a way of going unnoticed until the day after the boat is launched—when they are too dry for easy removal.

Exterior varnish is usually not necessary. Less expensive interior marine varnish is normally sufficient. Interior marine varnishes contain only minimal amounts of ultraviolet inhibitors, as they are intended for shaded areas such as cabin interiors. They will not stand up to strong sunlight through a clear glass windshield. One way to extend the life of interior varnish under these conditions is to put two or three coats of exterior varnish underneath two or more topcoats of interior satin varnish.

Stir Satin Varnish

When using satin varnish, forget the standard advice about never stirring varnish. Satin varnish contains a fine powder that creates the satin effect, and gravity causes this powder to settle to the bottom of the can. A fresh can of varnish should be stirred gently until all of the powder is suspended in the liquid. Every four or five minutes during application the can must be stirred again to keep the powder in suspension. Use a clean stick and stir slowly to prevent making air bubbles in the varnish.

The solvent that evaporates from varnish as it dries can create a stifling work atmosphere. A NIOSH-approved paint respirator makes breathing easier. Moreover, the solvent can reach explosive proportions in a confined area. Good ventilation of the cabin is mandatory for health and safety.

IMPROVING CABIN VENTILATION

Time: One to three hours per ventilator.

Materials: Vent grilles, deck ventilators, solar ventilators, bedding compound.

Tools: Drill motor, saber saw, drills, screwdriver, keyhole saw, hole saw.

Safety: Electric tool safety.

Nothing keeps a cabin smelling sweeter or prevents mildew better than good air circulation. The benefits of fresh air have been extolled by seamen for centuries. Yet most production boats are built with inadequate ventilation. Why? The answer is economics. Installing grates and ventilator ducts takes time and manpower, which translates into increased manufacturing costs. Boat builders don't like to spend money on features like ventilation that are not readily apparent to buyers. As a result, it's usually up to the owner to install extra ventilators.

Both Intake and Exhaust Are Necessary

In planning a ventilation system, keep in mind that there should be both a fresh-air intake and a stale-air exhaust. One ventilator working by itself is never as efficient as two working in tandem. Air needs an unobstructed pathway both to *enter* and to *exit* the area being ventilated. This intake-exhaust rule applies to the whole cabin, and to individual lockers within it as well.

There is no physical difference between a passive intake and a passive exhaust. They are identical and may actually alternate between roles depending upon the direction of the wind or almost imperceptible air currents. Active ventilators, which incorporate electric fans, are designed to be either an intake or an exhaust, depending upon the rotation of the fan.

Deck Ventilators

Polished brass or chrome air scoops were once the hallmarks of well-found yachts. Times have changed and boat decks have taken on the clean appearance of an automotive hood. The classic ventilator scoop has disappeared in the name of fashion. A traditional cowl ventilator on today's Euro-style boat definitely looks clunky and out of place. Fortunately, several manufacturers offer removable traditional cowl ventilators that can be replaced with waterproof deck plates. This type of vent can be left in place during the week while the

Thought must be given to the flow of air through the boat when planning a ventilation scheme. Here cowl vents have been combined with a louvered screen in the main hatch to provide moving air throughout the boat. Note that the cowls do not all face the same direction, so that some function as intakes while others work as exhausts. Good ventilation prevents mildew in all boats and helps fight dry rot in wooden boats.

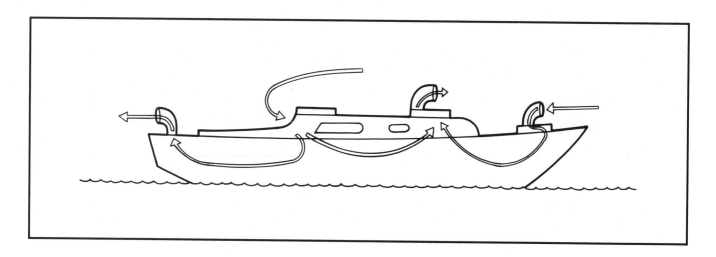

boat is not in use, then removed for good looks under way.

Cowl vents come with or without water separators. A water separator prevents spray or rain from finding its way down the vent and into the cabin. Integral water separators built into the vent are sufficient for powerboats and other craft where waves aren't expected to wash across the deck. Larger, wooden box separators (often called "Dorades," after a famous racing yacht) are suggested for sailboats. Neither type will keep all water out under the worst conditions. In really heavy weather cowl vents should be removed and the openings closed with watertight plates.

Here a chrome-plated bronze cowl (left) is being adjusted to provide the best ventilation. It is installed in the top of a teak water-separator box (called a "Dorade," after a famous racing yacht) to keep the cabin dry. This installation is typical of larger sailboats. The soft, plastic cowl vent is typical of smaller boats (right). This vent has a built-in water separator and screen. The plastic vent is used only when tied up in the dock. When out sailing, the boat's cowl is removed and replaced with a waterproof deck plate to keep water out of the forward V-berth.

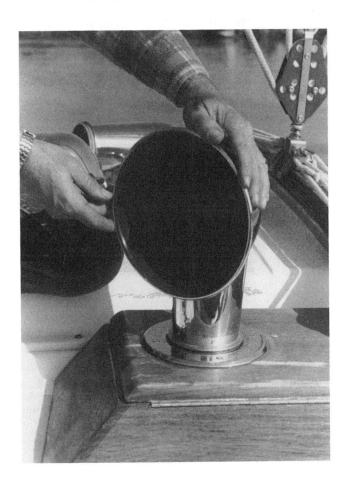

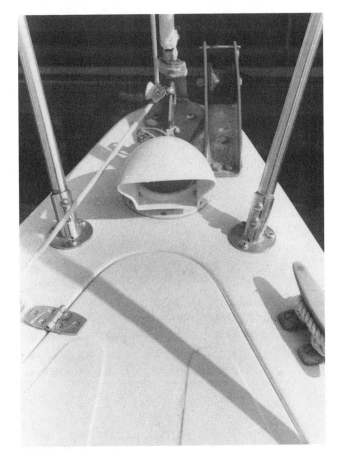

Several manufacturers offer "mushroom" ventilators. Their low profile allows them to be installed permanently on most boats without disturbing the aesthetic design. Built-in water separators are sufficient for keeping rain or spray out of the boat. In rough weather, mushroom vents can be made watertight by turning a handle on the inside of the vent. Mushroom vents of all-plastic construction will last several seasons before needing replacement. All stainless-steel vents have an indefinite lifespan. Vents with plastic bodies and stainless tops often break at the joint between metal and plastic.

Nicro-Fico produces a line of mushroom vents with built-in solar battery fans. During the day, the fans in these vents force stale air out of the cabin, resulting in a dramatic increase in ventilation. At night, the fans stop rotating, but the vents continue functioning in the same manner as a traditional passive mushroom vent. Because the fan is solar powered, it does not drain the boat's battery system when operating.

Installing Deck Vents

Exterior vents should be installed at opposite ends of the cabin or space they are to service. Place them as high as possible on cabin tops or protected decks. Follow the techniques outlined in Chapter 2 for drilling the necessary holes and bedding the ventilator base to prevent water leaks. Cowls should face in *opposite* directions, forcing one to become the intake and the other the exhaust. Normally, the cowls face fore and aft for best appearance, but there's no law against having them face athwartships to improve air flow.

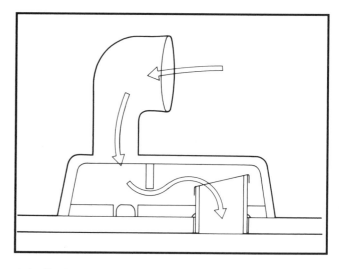

A baffled wooden box can be used to keep rain and spray from entering the cabin through a cowl ventilator. Air flows in an S-pattern through the box, while water comes out of the weep hole.

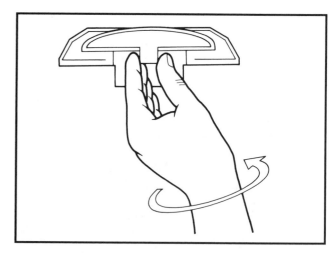

Mushroom ventilators are designed to be unobtrusive when installed in decks, hatches, or cabin sides. Made of metal or plastic, they have internal opening and closing mechanisms that work with a twist of the wrist. Some are also equipped with solar-powered fans that increase air flow during daylight hours. Mushroom vents are simple to install and good-looking even on modern, Euro-styled boats.

Locker Ventilation

Every closed space—every drawer, hanging locker, seat trap—is a potential mildew breeder. The more ventilation, the less mildew. Air circulation could be provided by drilling a series of 1-inch holes in every drawer front and cabinet door, but this would be flat ugly. Disguising ventilation holes so they blend into the boat's decor is part of the art of boatcraft. Here are a few proven techniques:

Metal Louver Vents: These come in a variety of sizes and shapes. Those of stainless steel look "finished" without painting. They are placed over the vent hole to block direct sight into the cabinet or locker. Metal louvers work well to ventilate seat lockers.

Plastic Louver Vents: Similar to metal louvers, but a bit less substantial. White plastic louvers blend well into the fiberglass interiors of most modern boats. Place them where they are not likely to be accidentally kicked or otherwise damaged.

Louvered doors allow plenty of air circulation within the lockers of this boat gallery while keeping the contents secure and out of sight. The same type of air circulation can be achieved with a pattern cutout in a solid door or by using commercially made metal or plastic vents.

Decorative Cutouts: Openings can be cut in cabinet doors that both ventilate the interiors and improve the appearance of the boat. Traditional patterns are sea gulls and anchors. Trace pattern on the door, then drill pilot holes for the coping saw.

Cane Door Panels: Caning of the type used on chair seats can be woven into a variety of patterns that look quite handsome in a traditional boat interior. Air circulates through the holes in the woven pattern, but the caning blocks sight of the contents of the locker. Open weave, man-made fabrics may be substituted for natural caning.

Finger Holes: Replacing traditional knobs or finger pulls on drawer fronts with finger holes can add ventilation to drawers. Finger holes are such an integral part of the drawer that they become almost invisible.

While there may be no such thing as too much ventilation, keep in mind that there can be too many ventilators. Louvers, cutouts, and caning should "disappear" in the overall cabin interior decoration.

INSTALLING A STEERING COMPASS

> **Time:** Sixty minutes.
>
> **Materials:** Compass, nonmagnetic fasteners, wire connectors.
>
> **Tools:** Drill motor, hole saw, drill bits, screwdriver, wire cutters, wire stripper, crimping tool.
>
> **Safety:** Electric tool safety.

The magnetic compass is the mariner's basic navigation tool. No boat larger than a dinghy should ever leave the dock without a properly installed and adjusted compass. Marine instruments available today are remarkably accurate devices. Problems of erratic or erroneous course display are almost always caused by improper installation. Mounting a steering compass is one of those times when it really pays to take pains to do the job absolutely right.

Choosing a Compass

Manufacturers offer what appear to be a bewildering variety of compasses. Marketing and style are partly responsible for the proliferation of compass designs, but other, more practical, factors are involved too. Designing a compass for a powerboat involves considerations not present in a sailboat design. Fast powerboats present additional problems. Some design features that should be considered in purchasing a compass include:

POWERBOATS

Vibration Dampening: Engine vibration and shock loads from the hull pounding into a head sea can affect compass accuracy. Better compass designs include special dampening to reduce or eliminate vibration problems.

Acceleration Dampening: The quick acceleration of modern performance boats can actually cause a compass card to spin. Acceleration dampening cancels out this spinning or reduces it to an acceptable minimum.

SAILBOATS

Full Gimbals: Sailboats can be expected to heel 30 degrees in normal weather and more than 45 degrees on occasion. Full gimbals allow the compass card to remain level no matter what the boat's angle of heel. Internal gimbals are less likely to be damaged than external gimbals.

Secondary Lubber Lines: These are additional lubber lines located at 45 degrees to the traditional lubber line aligned with the boat's keel. Secondary lubber lines allow the helmsman to steer an accurate course even when not seated directly in front of the compass.

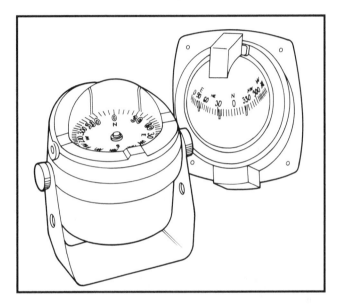

Boat compasses come in a wide variety of styles, but there are only two basic designs. One design mounts the compass in an external bracket that is attached to a vertical or horizontal surface. The other recesses the compass through a hole in the control console or cabin wall. The choice between these two designs is usually dictated by the location where the compass will be mounted.

Install the compass where it is easily seen by the helmsman. The lubber line of the compass must be aligned with the keel of the boat to prevent course errors. Avoid placing it near sources of magnetic interference, such as radio speakers or engine instruments. All 12-volt wiring near the compass should be twisted to prevent compass errors.

ALL BOATS

Compass Card Size: The larger the card, the more accurate the reading. A small, 2-inch card can be read with accuracy only in 5-degree increments. A large, 8-inch ship's compass can give accurate readings to half a degree.

Full-Sphere Bowl: Modern compasses are dampened by a thin oil contained in a "bowl." Fully spherical bowls allow movement of the fluid without whirls that might affect accuracy. Lower-cost compasses have a spherical front, but flat back side or bottom.

Built-in Adjusters: The accuracy of all compasses is affected by local magnetic influences on the boat. Small magnets can be used to adjust, or cancel out, the majority of these influences. Built-in adjusters have less effect than traditional external magnets, but are easier to use and solve the majority of compass error problems.

Magnet Size and Strength: Magnets, naturally, are the heart of the mariner's magnetic compass. Larger, stronger magnets are better. Most compasses actually have several magnets installed in a bundle beneath their cards.

Quadrantal Spheres: These are small spheres of iron installed on brackets to port and starboard of the compass binnacle. They are used to adjust the compass on a vessel made of steel or iron and are not needed on fiberglass or aluminum boats.

The location on the boat also influences the design of compass chosen. Freestanding binnacle-mount compasses can be installed on helm consoles or in traditional binnacle boxes. Wheel steering pedestals on sailboats have their own special compasses. Flush-mount compasses are intended for installation on vertical surfaces, such as helm consoles or sailboat cabin walls. When choosing a compass it pays to study the offerings of the major manufacturers.

Positioning the Compass

Three critical factors must be kept in mind when choosing the location for a compass:

1. The lubber line of the compass must be aligned absolutely parallel to the keel of the boat.
2. The compass should be located as far as possible from potential magnetic interference, such as radio speakers, engine instruments, and electrical wiring.
3. The helmsman should have good visibility of the compass without moving from his correct position at the steering wheel.

It should be immediately obvious that if the lubber line is not aligned parallel to the keel, the compass reading will not reflect the actual direction the boat is moving and accurate navigation will be impossible. Not quite as obvious are the detrimental effects of magnetic objects near the compass. Anything made of mild steel or iron and anything containing a magnet will have a profound influence on the compass. Lots of potential problems exist within the average powerboat console. Conventional analog engine instruments often have steel cases and permanent-magnet meter movements. All radio loudspeakers have permanent magnets. And, as if that's not bad enough, the current flowing through the wiring in the control console also sets up magnetic disturbances.

Fortunately, magnetic influences decrease rapidly with distance. A speaker magnet two feet away from the compass creates one-fourth the disturbance that it would at one foot away. Moving the disturbing material to above or below the level of the compass magnets also greatly reduces its influence. A few moments of careful thought can usually result in choosing a spot for the compass where magnetic disturbances will be the least. In the last resort, instruments and radio speakers can always be moved away from the compass.

The helmsman's line of sight should also get serious consideration. Ideally, he should be looking down on the card at a relatively shallow angle. Keep the whole crew in mind when choosing a location. If one of the potential helmsmen is a petite woman, her line of sight will be considerably below that of a six-foot male.

Installing the Compass

Nonmagnetic hardware should be used to fasten all compasses to the boat. High-quality stainless-steel screws, nuts, and bolts sold by marine stores are usually nonmagnetic. The same is true of copper, bronze, and brass screws. Never trust package labels, however. Check the magnetic influence of each fastener by bringing it near the compass. If there is any deflection of the card, discard that bolt or screw. Don't be surprised to discover shiny brass screws that have hearts of steel and only a thin plating of brass.

Also check any screwdrivers for magnetism. Many screwdrivers are magnetized so that they will pick up and hold steel screws. This feature is handy around the home but can lead to problems when installing a compass. Ghost magnetism from the screwdriver can be left behind in some stainless steel hardware. Then there's always the remote possibility that the magnetic tip of the screwdriver might alter or reduce the effectiveness

of the magnet bundles beneath the compass card.

Flush mounted compasses usually require drilling a sizable hole in the mounting surface. A hole saw in a ⅜-inch electric drill motor is usually the ticket. Consult the instructions before pulling the trigger on the drill motor. Most compass manufacturers provide full-size templates to guide the installation process.

Compasses mounted on the outside wall of a sailboat cabin must be sealed with bedding. Polysulfide compounds are usually a safe bet. Silicone products may damage some types of plastic used to house compasses. Polyurethane sealants should never be used, since the compass is almost surely going to be damaged should it ever have to be removed from the boat.

Wiring the Compass Light

Special care is needed when installing the small light to illuminate the card at night. Electricity flowing through a wire creates a magnetic field around that wire. Thus, a compass light is a potential source of trouble only when it is turned on. The classic way to prevent deflection of the compass is to twist the wires leading to the light around each other. Twisting the wires breaks up the magnetic field and forces it to cancel itself out.

Red bulbs are traditionally used in compasses to protect the helmsman's night vision. Recent research shows that while red is effective, any color light (including white) can be used without damaging night vision so long as it is sufficiently dim. No matter what the color of the light, the bulb in the compass should be only bright enough to allow reading of the numbers on the card.

UNDERSTANDING HEADS

Time: Ninety minutes to rebuild manual head; sixty minutes to clean holding tank.

Materials: Head repair kit, toilet chemicals, chlorine bleach.

Tools: Screwdriver, pliers, wrench, funnel.

Safety: Rubber gloves when working on head. Wash hands after pumping holding tank.

Working on either the marine toilet (also known as the "head") or the holding tank is everyone's least favorite job. Yet heads do need attention and holding tanks can develop unpleasant odors. There is nothing to do but roll up your sleeves, don rubber gloves, and get to work.

Understanding the Manual Head

The marine toilet is a marvel of simplicity. A single-piston pump both flushes the bowl and removes the waste. But because of this same simplicity, the marine toilet can also be cantankerous. There's a lot of truth in the old axiom that says, "Never put anything in the toilet that you didn't eat first." Cigarette butts, match sticks, and tampons are all guilty of plugging up the plumbing.

The only way to fix a plugged head is to take it apart. But before reaching for the wrench, take a minute to understand the internal workings. The operating lever (or rod) draws flush water into the top half of the pump. Pulling up forces this water into the ring around the top of the bowl where it flushes away the waste. The same up-and-down motion of the lever draws the waste into the bot-

tom of the pump and then forces it out the sewage hose to the holding tank. Several rubber valves are necessary to get all of that work done. Pump failures are rare, but these valves are subject to a variety of ills.

Rubber flapper valves control the flow of flush water through the top half of the pump. A small lever controls the operation of these valves. In one position, the pump operates normally; in the other position, the lever stops the pump from drawing flush water. This allows the bowl to be pumped dry. If flush water continues to flow regardless of the position of the lever, suspect these valves. Also, if these valves fail, raw water may be siphoned into the boat—and the boat can sink, if the head is located below the waterline.

Another set of valves controls the flow of waste through the pump. A large rubber flapper valve allows waste to be drawn from the bowl into the pump on the upstroke. It prevents waste from being sent back into the bowl on the downstroke of the operating lever. Suspect this valve if waste returns to the bowl on the downstroke.

The so-called joker valve is located on the waste outlet of the toilet. It has a well-earned reputation for refusing to pass anything that "wasn't eaten first." A joker valve problem usually prevents waste from leaving the bowl. Less often, a bad joker valve will allow waste to flow from the holding tank back into the toilet bowl.

Inside the pump is a single metal piston with a rubber ring that rides against the plastic pump-body wall. This ring forms the seal that prevents flush water from becoming contaminated with waste. If contamination occurs, the rubber ring needs replacement. A new ring is also indicated if the pump is difficult to operate.

All of the rubber parts needed to rebuild the pump and valves are available in kits. Match the kit with the model number of the head to insure that parts will fit. Rubber parts deteriorate over time. This deterioration is accelerated by exposure to sea water. Routine replacement every season or two will prevent a lot of unpleasant "head" aches.

Repairing the Head

Start by closing the sea cock on the raw flush water. Remove the drain plug in the base of the pump to dry down the mechanism. Have a sponge and bucket handy to sop up the water. Loosen and remove the flush-water hoses. The pump body can then be removed by loosening four bolts. Take it to a table for complete disassembly of the inlet valves and the piston.

Remove the knob from the piston rod and push the piston out the open bottom of the pump. Using a small screwdriver, pry the old O-ring off the piston and replace it with a new one. The water seal where the rod comes out of the pump body should also be pried out and replaced. A screwdriver will be needed to open the valve body and replace the flush-water flapper valves.

The waste flapper valve is located between the china bowl and the toilet base. It can be exposed by removal of the bowl. Replacing the joker valve requires removal of the valve housing, which serves as the waste outlet. Note the direction in which the old joker valve was installed. The new one must face the same direction or the toilet won't work.

The Holding Tank

Thanks to environmental legislation, the typical boat today is equipped with a 25-gallon chamber pot called a "holding tank." These tanks have no moving parts, so they don't require the sort of maintenance done on marine toilets. Odor buildup is the only serious problem requiring regular attention.

Holding-tank chemicals are supposed to control odors, and they do this reasonably well as long as the boat is sitting still. Once it begins to move, however, some waste is inevitably splashed onto the walls of the holding tank. This waste is not always fully treated, so bacterial action quickly begins producing an obnoxious odor.

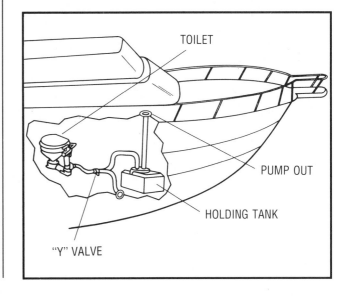

The best way to minimize this problem is to put off pumping the tank until it is nearly full. Contact with the chemical-laden waste tends to keep the walls clean. This is the reason why partly full tanks often have worse odor problems than full ones. It also pays to flush the tank after each pumpout. Flushing is done by filling the tank completely full with clean water and pumping it out a second time. This helps remove deposits from the walls right up to the top of the tank.

If the odor remains, try filling the tank with a mixture of clean water and holding-tank chemicals. On Sunday afternoon, fill the tank completely full, so that chemicals come in contact with all inside surfaces. Let the tank sit full for the week and pump it out the following Saturday morning. The odors should be gone.

Hose Problems

Waste hoses are often the source of odor problems associated with the boat toilet. Ribbed hoses can catch small bits of waste material, which are then able to decompose in the air. The joker valve is good at holding back liquids, but not smells. Before long, the toilet begins wafting an unpleasant aroma through the boat. This problem can be avoided by replacing ribbed waste hose with hose that is smooth inside.

Flush-water hoses can also be the source of unpleasant odors. These come from decomposing bacteria and plant life in raw sea water used to flush the head. Several manufacturers of marine toilets offer kits that insert metered amounts of deodorant and pump lubricant into the raw water used for flushing. Not only does this prevent odors, it also keeps the pump operating longer.

CHAPTER 6

SAILBOATS

Soaring masts and sails seem to rise out of a rat's nest of rope and rigging. Appearances, however, can be deceiving. There is order in this chaos. Seasoned sailors instantly recognize a vang from a sheet, or a snotter from a downhaul. Because of their complicated rigging, sailboats present unique maintenance and improvement opportunities.

RECAULKING THROUGH-DECK CHAINPLATES

Time: Fifteen minutes per chainplate.

Materials: Polysulfide, solvent, rags.

Tools: Screwdriver, ¼-inch chisel.

Safety: Care with sharp tools. Skin protection when using chemicals and solvents.

Chainplates are often stainless-steel bars that penetrate the deck to a bulkhead mounting below. This arrangement allows for narrow sheeting angles by placing the chainplates well inboard. However, the hole where the bar goes through the deck is always a potential source of leaks as a result of small movements of the chainplate relative to the hole when the boat is sailing. Flexible caulking is necessary to accept this movement while still blocking the entrance of water.

Polysulfide sealants are chosen for this job because they are relatively easy to remove when renewal becomes necessary. Polyurethane sealants last a bit longer in service, but are difficult to remove. Silicone materials don't have the lifespan for this application.

A decorative metal covering plate usually hides the exit hole of through-deck chainplates. This cover may be screwed down, but most are held in position only by the adhesion of the caulking beneath it. The tip of a screwdriver will usually pop it off the deck. Slide the cover up the chainplate and hold it out of the way with a small piece of masking tape. It is not necessary to remove the standing rigging from the chainplate.

Old caulking must be reefed out before new can be applied. A ¼-inch wood chisel works well, although a small electrician's screwdriver may work better if clearance is tight. Reef out as much of the old caulk as possible. Fill the opening with new sealant until the bead of caulking stands slightly proud above the deck. Let the cover plate slide back down into position and "squish" it around slightly to be sure it is firmly seated in the still-wet caulking. Wipe up any excess sealant with a rag and solvent.

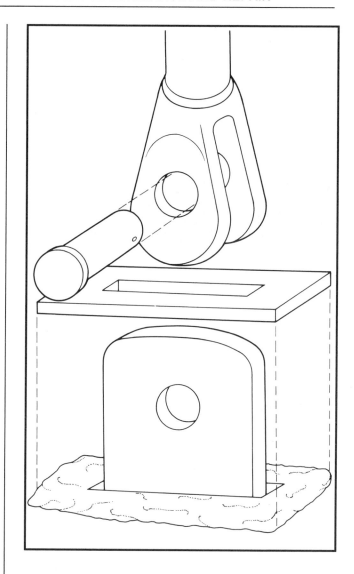

Leaking chainplates cannot be fixed by only smearing on clear silicone sealant. The real fix requires lifting the square metal plate around the fitting and replacing the polysulfide caulking beneath it. Some plates are held in place by small screws. Recaulking requires the removal of the screws and lifting the plate.

DRYING WEEPING KEEL BOLTS

Time: Fifteen to thirty minutes per bolt.

Materials: Polysulfide or polyurethane sealant, solvent, rags.

Tools: Wrench, wood chisel, screwdriver.

Safety: Skin protection when using solvent.

Sailboats often have external ballast keels of lead or cast iron that are held in place by large bolts. After a few seasons it is normal for one or more of these bolts to begin weeping. ("Weeping" is a sailor's term for a minor leak.) Weeping occurs at first when thrashing to weather. Later, the bolts weep even when the boat is at rest. Small leaks of this type aren't likely to sink the boat, but they can make life miserable.

Keel bolts come up through both the bottom of the boat and special floor timbers (or a grid structure) designed to spread the weight of the keel. Large fender washers and nuts on the inside of the hull draw the keel tightly to the boat. Copious quantities of sealant (usually polyurethane) are used to keep water out of the sandwich between the metal of the keel and the fiberglass laminate of the hull. More sealant is squirted around the bolts to keep water from climbing up the threads.

Minor leaks are often the result of almost infinitesimal loosening of the nuts due to the normal strains of sailing. Also, most boats change shape slightly once they are launched. These small shifts can often be accommodated by retightening the keel bolts a week or so after the boat has been launched. This may be all that's needed on a new boat to end weeping.

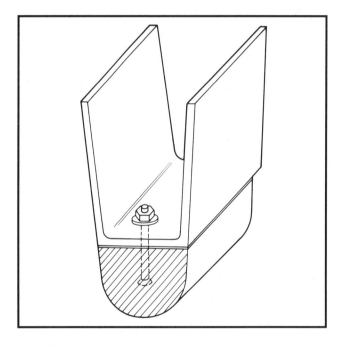

Bolts are used to hold an external metal keel to the hull. The joint between the hull and the keel should be sealed with plenty of caulking, as should the keel bolts themselves. Large nuts and washers inside the boat are used to draw the keel tightly against the hull. Water can weep into the boat via the keel bolts if they are not snug, or if the caulking is insufficient or deteriorated.

Keel bolts can be tightened from inside the boat even when it is afloat. A torque wrench can be used to keep track of the amount of torque on each nut. Changes in torque are clues that bolts are loose. Most people use a conventional box wrench or socket wrench.

Water seeping up the bolt threads can be stopped by recaulking each individual bolt, one at a time. Don't loosen more than one bolt at a time or the keel may part company from the boat. Clean out the old caulking beneath the fender washer, then recaulk and replace the nut. This process can be done with the boat either in the water or stored on shore.

If a major leak is discovered, the only solution is to haul the boat and drop the keel. A large boat lift and an oversize floor jack are needed—equipment not in the average family garage. Take the boat to a yard that knows sailboats. Separating

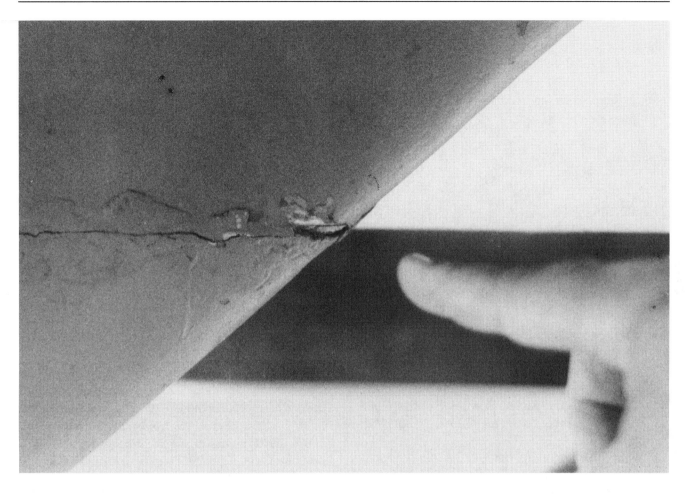

keels from hulls is heavy and dangerous work best left to professionals with both the knowledge and the equipment.

Once the keel is separated, the old caulking will have to be removed. This is a part of the job the average boat owner can do, if yard rules allow. At this point it pays to check the hull laminate and any floor timbers or internal grid structures for delamination or other problems caused by water leaks. Weeping or leaking keel bolts may be the symptom of deeper trouble. If everything is okay, new sealant should be applied to the keel and the bolts drawn up tight.

A small crack such as this one indicates the line where the cast iron keel is attached to a fiberglass hull on a sailboat. A crack may be a sign of loose keel bolts, or it may just indicate that the fairing compound covering the joint needs renewing. If the bolts are tight, all loose or cracked fairing material should be removed and replaced with an epoxy putty. Sand the putty smooth when it hardens and finish with antifouling paint.

GIVING THE MAST A BOOT

Time: Two and a half hours.

Materials: Kraft paper, synthetic canvas in same color as sail covers, nylon cord, Velcro strips or snap fasteners.

Tools: Sewing machine, large shears, spiling compass, pencil.

Safety: Care with shears.

Keel-stepped masts normally come equipped with waterproof boots to seal the hole where they pierce the cabin top. Original equipment boots generally last several seasons, but eventually they develop cracks and leaks. Polysar Rubber Corporation has just introduced an interesting solution to this problem.

Polysar is one of many companies that produce self-adhering rigging tape. Theirs is sold under the name Mariner's Choice. This tape does not have a "sticky" side. Instead, it has an unusual chemical composition: Stretching rigging tape against itself causes the surfaces to bond together on the molecular level. This bond keeps the tape securely in place, yet it can be easily unwrapped. Rigging tape is normally sold in 1-inch-wide rolls. Field reports say that Polysar's mast-boot tape is a real winner. Wrapping the average mast takes less than three minutes and the tape stays waterproof indefinitely.

Create a Decorative Boot

While modern boots are quite effective, they have a decidedly "generic" rubber appearance that does little to add to the overall visual appeal of the boat. A decorative mast boot cover made of the same material as the sail covers adds a dramatic touch of color. Sewing one starts with the creation of a kraft paper pattern. Traditional "cut-and-try" is simple enough when working with a paper pattern. Transfer this pattern to the synthetic canvas, then add sufficient margin all around to account for hems.

The top and bottom of the decorative cover should have nylon draw cords sewn into small tubes. These draw cords are used to tie the cover to the mast and the deck fitting. The concept is similar to the draw cords sewn into sweatshirt hoods. Velcro strips should be sewn into the ends of the cover so they can be joined into a continuous circle around the mast. If Velcro is not available, marine-grade snap fasteners are an acceptable alternative.

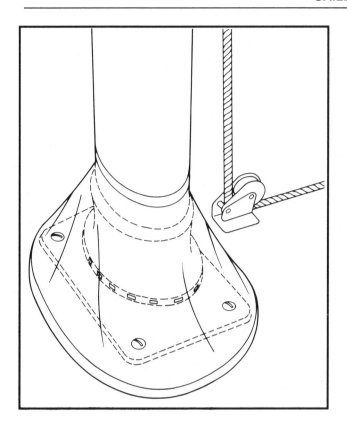

A decorative mast boot improves the appearance of a keel-stepped mast. Made of woven fabric, it does not waterproof the opening in the deck. That is the job of a rubber gasket. Instead, the boot serves a purely decorative function. It can be sewn out of Dacron canvas on most home sewing machines.

REPLACING MASTHEAD SHEAVES

Time: Forty-five minutes.

Materials: New sheave, new cotter pin.

Tools: Pliers, screwdriver, drift punch, hammer.

Safety: Eye protection if using drift punch.

Masthead halyard sheaves come under tremendous strain when sails are hoisted. Eventually, this strain takes its toll on the bearing where the sheave rotates on its axle. The first hint of trouble is a squealing sound aloft that sets the hair on the back of your neck on end. Replacing the worn sheave is the only repair, as it is usually not practical to drill out the center hole and install a bushing. The axle bolt seldom needs replacement. New sheaves are available either from well-stocked chandleries (and a few catalogue outlets) or directly from the manufacturer of the spar.

Removing the old sheave is easiest with the mast unstepped and horizontal on the ground. Masthead designs vary as to the method of disassembly. Most require removing a cotter pin from the axle and driving the axle out of the masthead to release the sheave. Be sure to have a good grip on the old sheave or it will disappear down the mast extrusion. All tension should be removed from the halyard when the sheave is being removed. It should not be necessary to remove the halyard from the mast.

Use the old sheave as a sample when purchasing a new one. Four dimensions are critical:

Outside Diameter: This is the maximum outer diameter of the sheave. Internal clearance of the masthead fitting normally limits outside diameter to less than 3 inches.

Bore Diameter: This is the diameter of the hole into which the axle fits. Common diameters are ¼, ⅜, ⁷⁄₁₆, and ½ inch.

Rope Score: The "score" is the depression in the outer rim of the sheave where the rope rides. The score must match the size of the rope being used. Sheaves of the same outside diameter may have widely different scores.

Wire Score: Similar to the rope score, but smaller in diameter and often inset into the rope score. The size of the wire score must be correctly sized to the diameter of the wire halyard being used.

Sheaves are made of a variety of materials including aluminum, UV-stabilized Delrin, and glass-filled nylon, sold under the trade name Marelon.

Installation of the new sheave is the reverse of removing the old one. A surgical hemostat makes holding the new sheave in position a lot easier. Hemostats are self-locking pliers of very fine dimensions that are easy to use in confined areas. Look for them in specialty tool stores or electronics outlets such as Radio Shack.

Masthead fittings do their work a long way from the cockpit. Close inspection and supervision is not possible during the sailing season. Never reuse a cotter pin at the masthead. Always replace old pins with new ones just for the feeling of security it gives. Also, be sure to use stainless-steel cotter pins and not common steel ones.

AVOIDING COMPRESSION-TUBE DEATHTRAP

Time: n/a

Materials: None.

Tools: Wrenches, pliers, screwdriver.

Safety: Maintenance and repairs to tangs should only be done with the mast unstepped and horizontal on the ground.

Mast tangs are the metal strap fittings to which shrouds and stays are attached. Tangs are seldom damaged, and even more seldom do they exhibit serious wear. As a result, most sailors are unfamiliar with just how tangs are attached to aluminum mast extrusions. When they do have to repair a tang, this unfamiliarity lets them fall into the infamous "compression-tube deathtrap."

Shroud tangs are set in pairs, one on each side of the mast. Large through-bolts are used to hang each pair of tangs because these fittings carry enormous loads when the rig is up and tuned. Using bolts solves the load problem, but it raises the possibility that the mast walls will be collapsed when the nuts holding the tangs are tightened. So, a compression tube is placed inside the mast to resist this inward pressure. The through-bolt slides through this tube.

Here's the deathtrap: Some compression tubes are not attached to anything inside the mast. They are kept in position *only* by the through-bolt. If that bolt is removed, the compression tube may come adrift and disappear down the mast extrusion. Getting a compression tube back into position can tax the patience of a saint. Rather than learn the mysteries of replacing a missing tube, don't let the

problem arise in the first place. Always put a "keeper bolt" or a wire through the compression tube whenever the tang bolt is removed.

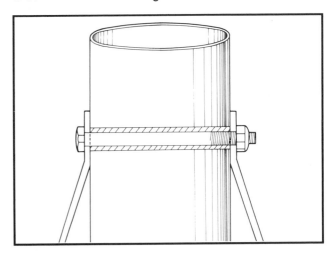

Some small sailboat masts use a compression tube around the bolt on which the shroud tangs are mounted. This tube prevents the aluminum mast extrusion from being collapsed by pressure from tightening the mounting bolt. Often this tube is held in place only by the bolt, so it will disappear down the mast if the bolt is withdrawn. Attaching a string to the bolt will prevent the loss of the compression tube when repairs are made to the tangs.

ANNUAL WINCH MAINTENANCE

Time: Forty-five minutes per winch.

Materials: White waterproof grease.

Tools: Screwdriver or wrench (varies with winch brand).

Safety: No special dangers.

Sail-handling winches lead a hard-knocks life. They are constantly exposed to the weather and are regularly doused with sea water; and the hot sun bakes the lubrication out of their bearings. It's a testimonial to good engineering and fine workmanship that sail winches give so little trouble. An occasional cleaning and lubrication will keep halyard or sheet winches working almost indefinitely. But because winches give so little trouble, maintenance is often forgotten until problems develop.

Basic winch maintenance involves removing the drum, cleaning the bearings, inspecting the pawls, and lubricating everything before reassembly. Although the job sounds simple enough, it can be intimidating with multiple-speed winches. Don't do any work without an exploded diagram of the winch showing how the parts go together. Write to the manufacturer for this drawing and a set of maintenance instructions.

Single-Speed Winches

Single-speed winches are relatively easy to clean and lubricate. They are just a drum that revolves on ball, needle, or sleeve bearings. One or more sets of spring-loaded ratchet pawls allow the drum

to rotate in only one direction. Pawls like to jump overboard when the drum is removed. That's why winch manufacturers sell spare parts. More important, that's why prudent sailors buy spare parts.

Removing the drum is usually a matter of loosening a retaining nut or screw in the center of the handle recess on top of the drum. Some winch drums (old Lewmar drums, for example) are kept in place by a circular retaining clip around the handle recess. Lift the drum straight off its base after the retainer is removed. Exercise caution so that those spring-loaded pawls don't fly out.

With the drum removed, all of the bearings, pawls, springs, and other working parts are fully exposed. Clean off any grease that has hardened into the consistency of an old bar of soap. Hard grease lubricates nothing. Remove as few parts as possible to clean out the old grease. Do not soak ball or needle bearings in solvent unless the equipment to properly repack them is available. Use fingers to work new grease into the bearing races or to smear a film of grease on the main sleeve bearing.

Winch manufacturers sell excellent greases for their products. Automotive wheel-bearing grease or other heavy greases should be avoided, as they may prevent the pawls from ratchetting properly in

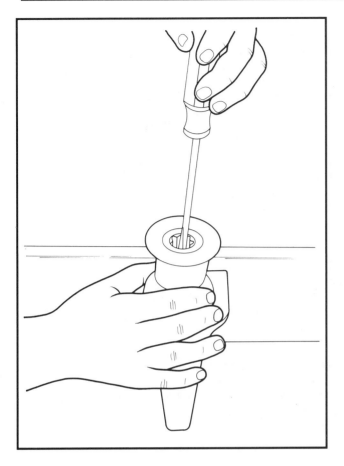

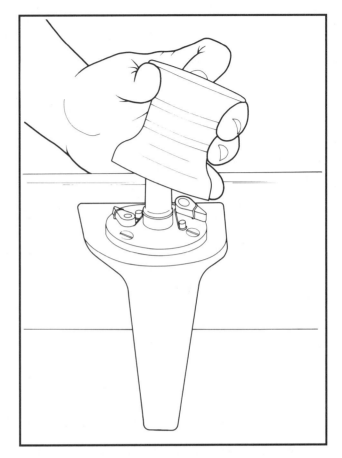

The first step in greasing a winch is to remove the drum. Start by loosening the retaining screw, which is recessed in the winch handle hole on top of the drum of most winches. Some manufacturers use a retainer ring around the handle hole instead of a screw.

Once the retaining screw is loose, the drum can be lifted off the winch base. Lift carefully to keep the spring-loaded pawls from flying overboard. The two pawls of this winch are clearly seen attached to the base.

the cogs of the drum. True winch grease is thin enough to allow the pawls to snap into place as the drum turns. But viscosity isn't its only special characteristic; winch grease is also highly resistant to heat. Temperatures inside the winch drum on a hot, sunny day can soar to the point that ordinary grease melts and runs out of the bearings. Good

winch grease is able to take the heat and stay on the job.

Winch pawls and their springs should be inspected carefully. Look for unusual wear that would indicate the pawl might not catch properly on the cogs. Formed wire springs have a habit of breaking one leg so that their force on the pawl is

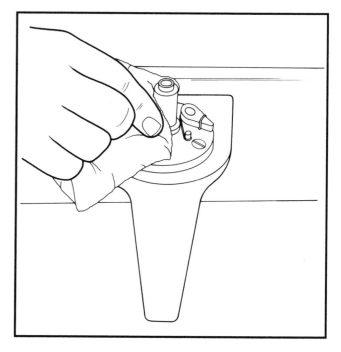

Hardened grease the consistency of soft soap no longer lubricates and must be replaced. A clean rag should be used to wipe hardened grease off the bearing surface of the center spindle, the pawls, and springs.

Closeup of winch drum and winch base showing the pawls and the cogs on the drum. These combine to allow rotation in only one direction. Worker's index finger points at one of the pawls. Inspect the cogs, pawls, and pawl springs carefully for unusual wear or damage. Pawls and springs often need replacement and are available in spare parts kits.

cut in half. The only repair is replacement. Once everything is pronounced okay, put the pawls back in position and carefully lower the drum onto its base.

Getting the pawls to retract into the drum usually takes a bit of trying. Rotate the drum slowly while nudging each pawl into place. Nothing will seem to fit until quite suddenly the drum will drop into its normal position. Replace the retaining screw, bolt, or clip and the job's done.

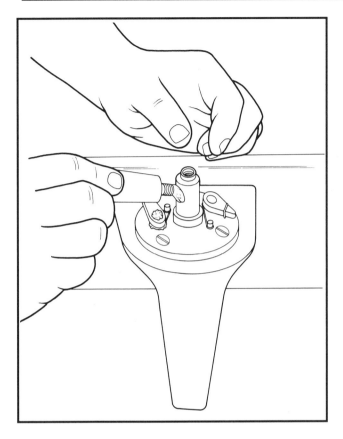

Special winch grease should be applied to all bearing surfaces and to the pawls. Winch grease is designed to withstand both salt water and high temperatures. Ordinary grease can melt and run out the base of the winch on a hot, sunny afternoon.

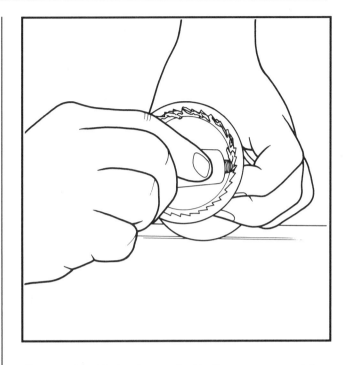

Grease should also be applied to the cogs around the inner perimeter of the winch base. A large amount of grease is not necessary. The goal is to get a thin film on all of the working parts, not large gobs.

Multiple-Speed Winches

Two- and three-speed winches are complicated devices. No single set of instructions can possibly apply to all of the various brands and models. Contact the manufacturer for instructions on disassembling and greasing the winch in question. Ask for an exploded diagram showing all of the various parts.

CHAPTER 7

ELECTRONICS AND ELECTRICITY

Electronics are the most popular boating accessories. At any chandlery, buyers are always crowded around the latest GPS receiver or videograph fish finder. Solid-state electronics and computer modules have brought high-tech to even the smallest boats. Most of the equipment available today performs as promised—but only if it is properly installed.

This chapter is not meant to replace the manufacturer's installation instructions that accompany any specific piece of equipment. Rather, it is intended to be a set of tips and guidelines to make following those instructions a bit easier.

While not specifically electronics, lightning protection and dockside AC power are also included here. Both are closely related, especially lightning protection, which can save a lot of expensive gear from an early demise.

PL-259 MAKES RADIO TALK POSSIBLE

Time: Fifteen minutes.

Materials: PL-259 coaxial connector, adaptor, solder.

Tools: Knife, wire cutters, wire stripper, soldering iron.

Safety: Cutting tool safety. A hot soldering iron may cause severe burns. Eye protection recommended when soldering.

A special connector, known as a PL-259, is used on the end of VHF-FM radio antenna wires. It maintains the coaxial configuration of the antenna wire right into the innards of the radio set. This is necessary to prevent any loss of transmitting signal strength. PL-259 connectors are available from stores selling marine radios as well as from electronics specialty outlets like Radio Shack. Although there are slight external differences between PL-259 connectors produced by different manufacturers, they will all attach properly to standard radio transceivers.

As it comes out of the package, the PL-259 connector is intended for RG-8 coax cable. This is large-diameter coax used on long runs where signal loss along the wire would be significant. RG-8 is seldom used on boats. More common is RG-8X cable, which is approximately ¼ inch in diameter. A special UG-255 adaptor must be screwed into the body of the PL-259 connector when the smaller diameter RG-8X coax is used. This adaptor is often sold separately from the basic connector. Other adaptors are available to fit coax cables used on a variety of electronics gear.

The PL-259 connector is composed of two parts: the connector body and the coupler ring. This ring can be unscrewed from the body when soldering the coax to the body. Note that the ring has a knurled pattern at one end and polished metal at the other. The knurled end of the ring always goes toward the tip of the body and the polished metal toward the coax wire when the two parts of the connector are assembled.

Start by cutting the end of the coax square with a sharp pair of wire cutters. Disassemble the PL-259 and push the coupler ring a short way down the wire. Be sure the knurled end of the ring is *toward* the cut end of the wire. Push the UG-255 adaptor onto the coax so that the large "collar" goes on first. The small end of the adaptor should be toward the cut end of the coax.

Using a knife, carefully slit around the outer insulation of the coax cable. The slit should be slightly over ⅝ inch from the cut end of the coax. Work carefully so as not to damage the braided shield that lies just beneath the outer insulation. Pull the insulation off and discard it. Slide the adaptor up the cable until it lies flush with the end of the plastic insulation. Fold the braided shield back over the end of the adaptor, cutting the braid so that it does not cover the threaded section of the adaptor. Using wire strippers, remove the insulation from ½ inch of the center conductor of the coax. Screw the adaptor into the back end of the PL-259 body.

The soldering iron should have been plugged in to heat up before beginning work. Irons work well for soldering PL-259, as do soldering guns. Be sure to purchase only *resin core radio solder*. Do not use plumbing solder and absolutely *never* use plumbing soldering paste. The corrosive nature of plumbing soldering paste causes high-resistance connections, which severely limit radio transmitting power. Radio solder uses a special resin flux that is contained in the hollow core of the solder.

Installation of a PL-259 coaxial plug must be done with care to insure maximum radio performance. Start by sliding the coupling ring and the UG-255 adaptor onto the antenna coax. Then remove the plastic insulation for a distance of just under ¾ inch. Turn the woven metal braid back over the insulation. Push the adaptor into the braid. Skin the center conductor of the coax for a distance of ½ inch. Slide the body of the PL-259 over the center conductor and screw it onto the UG-255 adaptor. Solder the center conductor of the coax to the center post of the plug. Use a drop of solder in one of the holes in the plug to make a good electrical contact between the braided shield and the PL-259 body. Screw the coupling ring back onto the plug body.

This resin does not interfere with the electrical qualities of the joint.

Solder the center wire of the coax to the center post of the PL-259. Apply the heated soldering iron to the wire's end and then lightly touch the solder to the wire. Apply just enough solder to coat the connection evenly. The wire should be sticking through the center post if the coax has been installed correctly. Use only enough heat to melt the solder. Excessive heat will damage the coax insulation, possibly leading to a short. Let the solder cool before snipping off any excess wire extending beyond the center post.

The body of the PL-259 has two holes located 110 degrees apart through which the braided shield of the coax should be visible. Working carefully, solder the shield wires to the connector body through these holes. Allow the connector to cool. The coupling ring is now screwed onto the body of the connector. Continue turning the ring until it is completely past the threaded section of the body. The ring should now be "captive" on the body, yet free to rotate.

It takes a special piece of test equipment to check continuity on a VHF-FM antenna. A practical test of a newly soldered PL-259 is to push the center post into the antenna connection on the back of a radio set. Be sure neither the outer body of the PL-259 nor its coupling ring touch the radio. Tune to a weak signal. Push the connector ring up so that it contacts the back of the set. There should be a noticeable improvement in signal strength. If there is no improvement, suspect a bad solder connection. Or, if the radio can acquire no signals whatsoever, suspect a short in the PL-259.

PRO TIP

PL-259 coax connectors don't last long in the marine environment, especially around salt water. Internal corrosion is a prime factor in loss of transmitting power and/or reduced ability to receive weak signals. Installing a new connector every other season is good insurance against signal loss. Connectors exposed to the weather or excessive salt water may need replacement more often.

FIXING BROKEN ANTENNA MOUNTS

Time: Forty minutes.

Materials: New mount fixture, bedding, nuts and bolts.

Tools: Wrench, screwdriver, pliers, putty knife.

Safety: Hand tool safety.

Swivel-mount bases for VHF-FM antennas have the annoying habit of breaking. Nylon plastic mounts fail most often, but even metal ones will snap if put under enough unfair strain. There is no easy way of repairing a broken mount. Replacement is almost always necessary. This is a pretty straightforward job, with the only complication coming from the coaxial cable that connects the antenna to the radio set.

Remove Broken Parts

The first step is to remove the antenna from the broken mount. More than likely, the mount is already in two pieces. If not, loosen the adjusting handle on the mount and remove the bolt through the fixture. The mount should now be in two pieces, one of which will be attached to the deck and the other to the antenna. A short section of coax will come out of the piece of the mount attached to the antenna.

In traditional installations, the coax runs from the center of the antenna through a hole in the middle of the antenna mount. This means that the top section of the mount is held captive on the wire. Newer antennas allow the coax to exit the antenna at the side so that it does not have to be passed through the center of the mount.

The antenna is then unscrewed from the top half of the mount. Ordinary hand pressure may be sufficient to separate the two. Wrenches are often needed, but use caution not to damage the fiberglass section of the antenna. Always keep the antenna from rotating while the top half of the base is rotated until it comes off the antenna. This helps prevent damage to the coax from excessive twisting.

If the upper half of the base is captive on the coax, the wire must be pulled out of the old piece. Pulling out the wire requires cutting the PL-259 connector off the end of the coax near the radio. The coax is then slowly pulled out of the boat and up through the base of the mount. This time-consuming step is not necessary with the newer, side-exit antennas.

The bottom half of the antenna mount is normally bolted to the deck with four 1/4-20 bolts. Large lag screws may also be used but are less common. Remove the bolts or screws and set them aside for reuse in installing the new base. The lower half of the old base can now be lifted off the deck. Discard the broken section of the old base, but save the rest of the pieces as spare parts.

Installation Is the Reverse

Installation of the new antenna mount is essentially the reverse procedure. Use a silicone or polysulfide sealant to prevent water from leaking into the boat around the bolt holes. Also put a good dollop of sealant around the coax where it comes out of the deck or cabin side. If the old PL-259 antenna connector was cut off, replace it with a new connector.

INSTALLING A VHF-FM TRANSCEIVER

Time: Two hours.

Materials: Radio set, antenna, antenna mount, through-deck cable feed, hookup wire, polysulfide bedding, radio solder.

Tools: Electric drill motor, drill bits, screwdriver, wire stripper, wire cutter, pliers, wrench, soldering iron.

Safety: Use caution with hot soldering iron.

Electronics manufacturers have gone a long way toward "idiot-proofing" the installation of a VHF-FM marine radiotelephone. Anyone familiar with 12-volt electrical systems should be able to get the job done. However, it is not a job to undertake lightly. Mistakes can reduce transmitting range or even cause disabling internal damage to the radio. Read the instructions that come with the radio before opening the tool box. Start work only after you have read fully and understood the instructions.

The radio should be located where it can be operated easily by the helmsman. Overhead electronics boxes are popular on flying bridges and center-console boats. Beware of interference with the steering compass if the radio is to be installed within the helm console. Speakers in radios use strong magnets which can cause compass deviation.

Voltage is critical to radio transmitter operation. A small voltage drop translates into a larger than expected drop in power output at the antenna. Use Table 2.6, "Critical Applications," in the section on 12-volt wiring in Chapter 2, page 61, to choose the size of power-feed wires. The radio may be wired into the boat's "instrument" circuit if that circuit has enough power available. However, it is better to wire the radio directly to the output of the main 12-volt battery switch. This insures adequate power for full transmitting output.

Like all other electrical equipment, a VHF-FM radio requires overcurrent protection in the form of a fuse or circuit breaker. The power cord included with most sets is wired with an in-line fuse holder in the positive (+) lead. Be sure to use the fuse specified in the instruction manual.

Antenna Installation

Antennas are deceptively simple. Inside that white fiberglass stick is a carefully tuned electronic device. VHF-FM antennas are quite different electrically from those intended for citizens band or Loran-C equipment. Using the wrong antenna will severely limit reception of distant stations. Worse, it may create what radio engineers call "standing waves" in the antenna. Standing waves are ca-

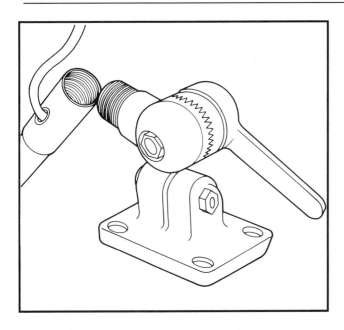

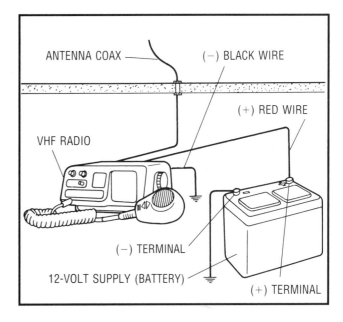

The VHF antenna threads onto the base. The coax cable exits the antenna from the side of the fiberglass whip above the threaded recess of the antenna. Avoid twisting or kinking the coax when screwing the antenna onto the base.

Hooking up a VHF marine radio involves connecting both the power and the antenna. Use the table of "Critical Applications" (Table 2.6, page 61) when choosing wire for the 12-volt supply. Low voltage caused by undersize wiring can significantly reduce transmitting range. The red (+) lead should be protected with a fuse or connected to a circuit breaker in the main 12-volt power panel.

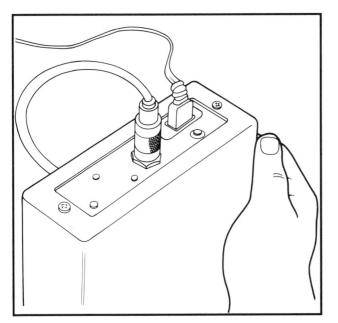

Connections on the back of a typical VHF-FM marine radio transceiver are easy to figure out. The round threaded connector is a PL-258, which receives the PL-259 plug on the antenna coax. Next to it is a flat connector for the 12-volt power supply. This plug is shaped so that it can only be inserted one way, insuring correct polarity.

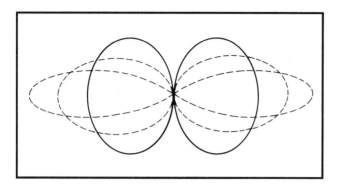

High-gain antennas concentrate the transmitting power into a narrow band. This increases range since more of the power goes toward distant receivers. However, rolling motion of the boat can cause loss of contact as the output power is alternately focused on the sky and into the water. As a general rule, sailboats should use a 3 dB gain antenna for masthead mount. Powerboats can use a 6 or 9 dB gain antenna mounted on the deck or the cabin top.

pable of causing severe damage to the transmitting part of the radio. Always be sure the antenna is marked for use on the VHF-FM marine radio band.

Antennas have something called "gain," which is expressed in decibels (dB). For every 3 dB of gain, the effective power is doubled. Marine antennas typically have between 3 and 9 dB of gain. It might sound as if a 9 dB antenna is better than a 3 dB, but this is not always the case. To get gain, the antenna must compress the radiated power into a narrow beam. This is analogous to the mirror of a flashlight, which concentrates light from the bulb into a narrow beam.

As a general rule, antennas with a gain of 6 or 9 dB are suitable for powerboats or for deck mounting on a sailboat. If the antenna is to be mounted at the top of a sailboat mast, however, a 3 dB antenna will give better performance. Keep in mind that VHF signals are line-of-sight, no mat-

ter how much gain the antenna has. Raising the height of the antenna does more to increase range than does the gain of the antenna. A narrow-beam 9 dB antenna can actually cause communication problems from a rolling powerboat or a heeling sailboat.

Marine antennas have a permanently attached coaxial cable, which is connected to the radio. This cable must be led into the boat using a through-deck cable feed. Excess cable may be cut off, but leave 4 or 5 more feet than the absolute minimum length between antenna and radio. This allows for future movement of the radio or for the almost inevitable replacement of the PL-259 coax connector.

A PL-259 has to be soldered to the end of the coax once it has been led through the deck and to the radio. (See the section entitled "PL-259 Makes Radio Talk Possible," page 156, for full details.)

INSTALLING A DEPTH SOUNDER

Time: Two hours.

Materials: Depth sounder, transducer, wire, in-line fuse holder, crimp connectors, electrical tape, rubber grommet, self-tapping screws or bolts and nuts, polyurethane sealant. For inside-hull transducer: plastic pipe, pipe cap, pipe glue, mineral oil, epoxy putty.

Tools: Drill motor, hole saw, drill bits, saber saw, wire cutters, wire stripper, crimping tool, screwdriver, pliers, small wrenches.

Safety: Electric tool safety. Boat must be properly blocked on shore when working under the bottom.

Installation of a depth sounder involves two completely separate pieces of equipment connected by a special wire. One is the electronic (control) unit located near the helm station. Its installation is usually the easiest part of the job. The harder installation is the transducer unit. On most large boats the transducer is installed through the bottom of the boat and requires a beveled pad as well as care to waterproof everything. Transom-mounted transducers are common on smaller, or trailerable, boats.

The Control Unit

Most depth sounders are intended for bracket mounting on the helm station. Physical installation involves picking the right space, screwing down the bracket and then slipping the unit into place. Self-tapping screws are usually sufficient, although nuts and bolts are recommended if there is access to the underside of the helm console. Before drilling any holes, be sure the control unit does not interfere with either the magnetic compass or with the helmsman's view.

Some units are intended for flush mounting within the console. Installing one of these requires cutting a hole of the correct shape and size. Before drilling or cutting, find a piece of colored scrap paper. Snip out an exact silhouette of the instrument and then tape this paper mockup onto the console. Sit in the helm seat to be sure sight lines are okay. Look at the mockup from various locations in the boat to be sure that the unit won't appear obtrusive. Then check inside the console behind the mockup to be sure there's enough room for the instrument and its wiring.

Use the factory-supplied template as a guide when making the actual cutout in the console. This is typically done by drilling holes at the corners of the cutout and then connecting those holes with saw cuts made with an electric saber saw.

Depth sounders require three wires. One is the cable that connects the control unit to the transducer. The other two carry the 12 volts of power to the control unit. A fourth bonding wire may be

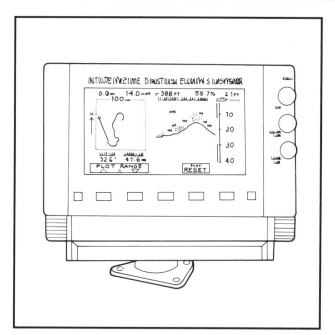

Most depth sounders and fish finders are surface-mounted in metal brackets. Bolting down the bracket is the simple part of the job. Running the 12-volt power wires and transducer cable so that they do not detract from the appearance of the boat is much more difficult.

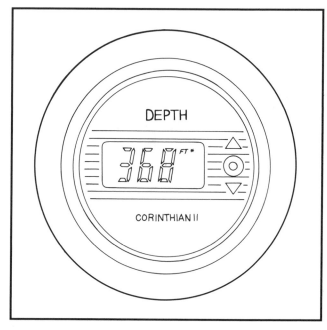

A flush-mounted depth sounder is recessed into the bulkhead or helm station console. Cutting the large hole for the instrument case requires careful use of a hole saw. The wiring of flush-mounted instruments is automatically hidden once the depth sounder is in place.

added but is not absolutely required. If used, the bonding wire should attach to the ship's grounding system. The transducer cable will be supplied by the manufacturer. Number 10 wire is usually acceptable for the 12-volt supply. Use red for the hot lead (+) and white or black for the negative (−) ground lead. If used, the bonding wire should be at least number 10, with green insulation.

Overcurrent protection must be provided. Instrument manufacturers usually include an in-line fuse holder in the 12-volt wiring supplied with the unit. This allows the depth sounder to be connected directly to the boat's power bus. The in-line

fuse holder is not necessary if the unit is wired to a circuit breaker or fused switch on the boat's instrument panel. Consult the unit's instruction manual to determine the proper size for the fuse.

A rather large hole is usually required to get all of the wires into the console. This hole always looks unfinished unless a rubber grommet is used. A grommet is just a rubber "doughnut" that protects the wires as they pass through. Grommets come in a variety of common sizes from ¼ to 1 inch. Look for them in a well-supplied marine electronics store or in electronics shops like Radio Shack. Drill a hole the proper size for the grommet, then wet the rubber (spit works great!) and "ooch" it into position. Feed the wires through the grommet after it is in place.

The Transducer

There are two different types of transducer installations: through-hull and transom. Transom-mount units are easy to install, especially on small boats. Unfortunately, the accuracy of readings from transom-mounted transducers is often compromised by air bubbles in the water stream passing under the boat at high speed. The proper installation of a through-hull transducer can be intimidating, which is why so many people pay a boatyard to do the job.

Most brackets for transom-mounted transducers allow adjustment to match the angle of the transom. The idea is to get the face of the transducer as close to parallel with the surface of the water as possible. Adjusting the threaded nuts on the transducer stem allows exact placement of the face of the transducer just below the waterline when the boat is planing across the water. Self-tapping screws are usually sufficient for attaching the bracket to the boat. Be sure to seal the threads with polyurethane sealant.

Through-hull transducers must be installed where they will always be in contact with a smooth flow of water across the bottom of the hull. The general rule is to install transducers in the forward third of sailboats where the flow is smooth and the signal from the transducer won't bounce off the keel when the boat heels. On powerboats, the after third of the hull is preferred, because it stays in the water even at planing speeds.

The transducer should always be mounted so that it points straight down at the bottom. Most boats have a deadrise angle, which must be taken into account with a beveled fairing block. The

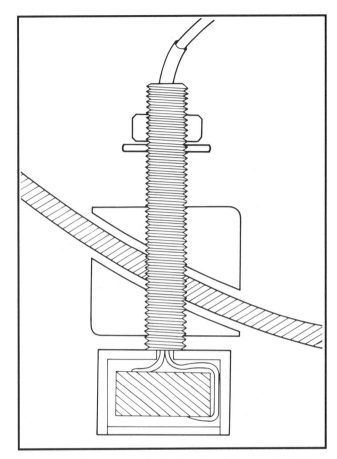

Provision must be made for the deadrise angle of the bottom when installing a through-hull depth sounder transducer. Otherwise, the transducer would point at an angle instead of straight down toward the bottom. Angling the transducer reduces its efficiency. A wood or plastic fairing block should be cut to match the deadrise angle. Half of this block is mounted outside the hull while the other half goes inside. Use lots of polyurethane sealant on all mating surfaces to prevent leaks.

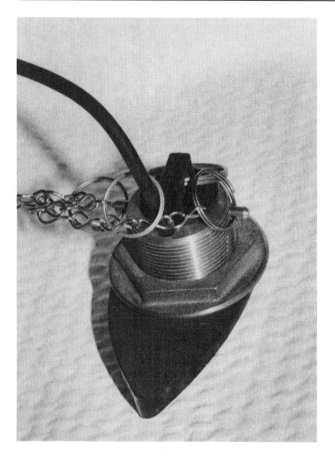

A typical through-hull depth sounder transducer seen from inside the boat. A boat-shaped fairing block accounts for the deadrise angle of the bottom. The jam nut keeps the bronze through-hull in place. This transducer is also a speedometer pickup. The black center section is the paddle wheel mechanism, which can be removed for servicing. It is kept in position by a stainless-steel pin that is attached to the small chain so it won't get lost.

The same transducer viewed from outside the hull. A boat-shaped fairing block is also used here to account for the deadrise angle of the hull. The paddle wheel mechanism would not be present in a transducer that is solely a depth sounder.

block should be shaped to the contour of the transducer, then cut horizontally at the same angle as the deadrise of the boat. The bottom half of the block is installed on the outside of the hull, while the top half goes inside. This provides a flat mounting surface outside for the transducer and inside for the retaining nut and washer.

Fairing blocks should be made of dense, rot-resistant wood such as teak, or, preferably, of plastic. Either material can be cut or drilled with ordinary woodworking tools. The deadrise angle is best cut on a bandsaw with the table tilted. Since a transducer is a permanent installation, polyurethane sealant should be liberally applied to all mating surfaces. Be sure to get sealant in the threads of the transducer stem where it goes through the fairing block and hull.

No-Holes Transducer

It is possible to install a transducer inside the hull of a fiberglass boat provided that the bottom does not have balsa wood or plastic foam coring. Fiberglass and resin are dense enough to pass the signal from the transducer to the water, although there will be some loss of power. The trick is to install the transducer inside a small section of plastic pipe filled with mineral oil. The oil transmits the output of the transducer to the fiberglass which puts the signal into the water.

Plastic drain pipe works well. Choose a pipe diameter large enough for the transducer body and cut a section just shorter than the overall length of the transducer. Using pipe glue, cap one end of the cut section so that the joint is watertight. Trim the open end of the pipe to match the curve of the hull. Drill a small hole at one side of the pipe cap and thread it for a small bolt. Drill a second hole for the transducer stem in the exact center of the

pipe cap and mount the transducer using polyurethane or polysulfide sealant.

Remove any paint or other coating from the area of the bilge where the pipe will be installed. It

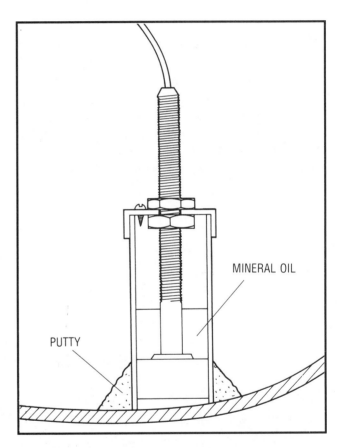

Solid fiberglass laminate is "transparent" to the high-frequency sound used by depth sounder transducers. This allows the transducer to be mounted inside the boat without drilling any holes in the bottom. A PVC pipe filled with mineral oil acoustically couples the transducer to the fiberglass hull. This technique will not work if the hull has any balsa or foam core material in the bottom.

is vital that the fiberglass be exposed and clean. Bond the pipe containing the transducer to the hull with epoxy putty, being sure to obtain a strong, watertight fit. When the epoxy has cured, use a small funnel to fill the pipe with mineral oil (or baby oil). Screw the bolt into the filler hole to keep the oil inside the pipe.

The Transducer Cable

The cable attached to the transducer is a type of wire designed especially for this purpose. It should never be cut or shortened, as this may affect the performance of the depth sounder. Route the cable as far away from engine ignition wires and fluorescent light fixtures as possible. If there is extra

cable, coil it up with wire ties and stow it in the bilge or inside the control console.

Eliminating Interference

Ignitions from outboard trolling motors and other on-board equipment can cause annoying interference for the depth sounder. Often called "sparkling" by anglers, interference obscures depth indication and fish returns. One cumbersome solution is to operate the depth sounder from a separate battery power supply. More practical is to install a low-pass filter in the power supply from the boat's regular battery system. This filter effectively isolates the depth sounder from the boat's electrical system and eliminates any interference.

LIGHTNING PROTECTION IS CRITICAL

Time: Two to six hours, depending on construction of boat.

Materials: Lightning rod, ground plate, electrical bonding conductors, crimp connectors, solder, mounting hardware, polyurethane caulk.

Tools: Electric drill motor, drill bits, screwdriver, pliers, wrench, wire cutters, crimping tool, soldering iron.

Safety: Observe caution when using spark-producing tools in the bilge, where explosive gasoline fumes may collect. Soldering irons may create a fire danger.

Lightning strikes boats with surprising frequency. Sailboats, with their tall aluminum masts, are little more than seagoing lightning rods. Don't think that your powerboat is exempt, however. Its signal masts and radar arches are high enough to attract lightning when surrounded by open water. Preventing lightning from striking is virtually impossible. Lightning safety on the water is, rather, a matter of protecting the boat and its human cargo from serious injury when lightning does strike. A "zone of protection" is created through the use of a lightning rod and a sophisticated grounding system.

SAFETY NOTE

Boats vary so widely in their design and construction that no one set of instructions can cover all situations. Basic guidelines such as American Boat and Yacht Council standard E-4 should be considered as just that—guidelines. Specific recommendations cannot be made to cover all possible situations.

The Air Terminal

Electrical engineers use the phrase "air terminal" to refer to what ordinary folks call a lightning rod. This is a conductive *metal* rod that terminates in a sharp point. It is normally mounted in the highest position on the boat to provide maximum protection. Rods are typically made of good electrical conductors, such as aluminum or copper, although any metal that conducts electricity will do.

For complex technical reasons, the rod should have a sharp point at its highest end. This point helps "guide" the lightning bolt to the boat's protection system.

A lightning rod creates what is called a "zone of protection," a cone-shaped space with the rod at its apex. The circular base of the cone has a radius equal to the height of the top of the lightning rod. Objects inside of the zone of protection are generally safe from lightning strikes. A rod at the top of a sailboat mast usually provides a zone of protection extending well beyond the ends of the boat. Conversely, a short signal mast on a powerboat may protect only a fraction of the hull.

Anything that extends *outside* of the zone of protection is obviously a target for lightning strikes. If adequate protection cannot be obtained from one lightning rod, two or more can be installed to provide overlapping zones of protection. A mizzen mast on a ketch or yawl obviously extends outside the zone of protection created by the main mast and needs its own protection.

The tip of the lightning rod should extend at least six inches above the top of the mast on which it is mounted. Fiberglass radio "whip" antennas may be considered as "air terminals" only if they and their coax leads have a conductivity equivalent to 8-gauge stranded copper wire. If the antenna has a loading coil, there must be a suitable protective device for bypassing the lightning current.

Often forgotten is the fact that people—specifically, their heads—can often stick out beyond the zone of protection. Walking around on deck (particularly at the ends of the boat) can expose a crew member to being struck by lightning even though the deck he is walking on is protected. During a lightning storm, crew members must stay within the zone of protection provided by the boat's lightning protection system.

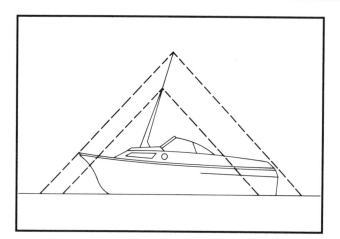

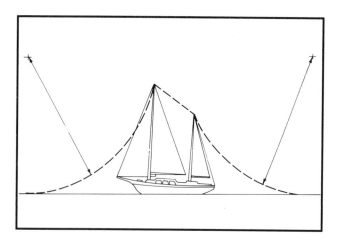

Lightning protection extends downward in a cone from the tip of the air terminal of the lightning ground system. Equipment and people inside the cone are protected from a direct strike. Depending on the height of the air terminal, however, the cone of protection may not cover the entire boat. Also, a fiberglass radio antenna may not provide any protection at all. On multi-masted vessels with masts over 50 feet tall, the zone of protection is no longer a simple cone. The dashed lines indicate the zone of protection based on a lightning strike from 100 feet away. For masts or other objects to provide lightning protection they must be connected to a properly designed grounding system.

Lightning Ground Plate

Lightning that strikes the boat's air terminal has to go somewhere. That's the purpose of the ground plate: to dissipate the electrical charge into the surrounding water. In the days of the old AM radiotelephones, most boats had large copper sheets attached to their hulls or keels to serve as radio grounds. These copper sheets also served as excellent ground plates. Ordinary 1-inch copper water pipe has also been used as a radio and lightning ground by bolting it to the keel. Today's smaller ground plates (the Dynaplate, for example) are acceptable, *provided that they have a surface area of at least one square foot.*

A ground plate, if it is to work, needs to be fully submerged at all times. That's why it is normally attached to a deep portion of the keel and not at the boat's waterline. Metal parts of the boat such as rudders, centerboards, and keels can do double duty as lightning grounds. Many boats are equipped with special ground plates to increase the effectiveness of their Loran-C receivers. These ground plates can also be used as the boat's lightning ground.

The importance of an adequate ground plate cannot be overstated. Fiberglass boats without ground plates have been sunk when struck by a lightning bolt. With no easy way to escape, the electrical charge literally blasts its way out of the hull. This creates dozens or even hundreds of holes ranging in diameter from the size of a pin to an inch or more. Vessels with metallic hulls may not require ground plates so long as their hulls are not electrically insulated from the water.

Interconnection Wiring

Special conductors are necessary to lead the lightning bolt safely through the boat from the air terminal to the ground plate. Bare copper braid is often chosen because it has no insulation to burn off when heated by the passage of large electrical currents. Individual wire conductors of either braid or stranded bare cable must be 17 gauge or larger. The total conductivity of the braid or cable must be equal to that of 8-gauge wire. Copper ribbon can also be used, provided that it is at least 1/32 of an inch thick.

Interconnecting wires should have as few splices as possible. All connectors must be installed with care, since a high-resistance joint may cause lightning to jump out of the protection system to some other part of the boat. Also, a high-resistance connection may get extremely hot when struck by lightning and ignite a fire. Crimp connectors are acceptable, but twist-on connectors (Wire Nuts, for example) are forbidden. Solder must not be the sole means of mechanical connection. All terminals should be eyes or captive lugs.

Large metal masses inside the boat should be connected to the lightning protection system. This is to prevent damage from "side flashes," which can jump gaps of up to 6 feet inside a boat. Typical large internal metal masses include fuel tanks, water tanks, steering gear, and transmissions. Engines deserve special consideration. Internal engine rod and crank bearings can be seriously damaged by a side flash that exits the boat via the prop shaft. To prevent bearing damage, it is recommended that engine blocks be connected directly to the ground plate rather than to any intermediate point on the lightning conductor.

External metal masses must be connected to the lightning grounding system to protect the crew. Typical hardware that must be connected include metal handrails or lifeline stanchions, metal grab rails on cabin tops, galley or cabin heater smokestacks, electric winches, dinghy davits, metal signal masts, and even metal hatches. Sailboats

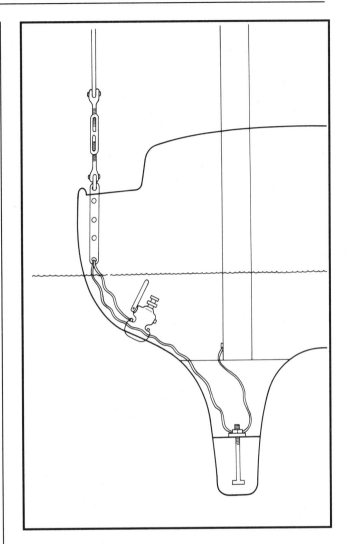

Sailboat rigging should be tied into the lightning ground system. Heavy copper cable should be used to connect the chainplates to the groundplate, which in this case is the boat's external ballast. The bronze sea cock in this drawing is also connected to the ground system because of its proximity to the chainplate. If it were not connected, the possibility might exist of a dangerous "side flash," in which lightning jumps from the ground system to the sea cock.

have special considerations. All masts, booms, metal shrouds, back stays, preventers, and continuous metallic track on wooden masts or booms must be connected. Likewise, deck-mounted winches, sail tracks and other metallic sail-handling equipment should be part of the lightning protection system.

Maintaining Protection

A lightning protection system is passive. Any problems caused by lack of maintenance won't show up until lightning strikes the boat with devastating consequences. Prudence calls for inspecting the entire system prior to launching the boat each spring. Pay particular attention to interconnecting wires that run in the lower portions of the bilge, where corrosion is almost unavoidable. Remember: A strong physical connection is no indication that the joint will conduct electricity. Lugs that are subject to bilge water should be removed from their terminals for inspection. Any corrosion on the stud or terminal should be removed with fine sandpaper.

All portions of the protection system should be inspected in detail if the boat is struck by lightning. Chances are, the lightning rod will be burned and portions of the interconnecting wires damaged. Pay particular attention to the continuity of the system to the surrounding water. Compasses and electrical and electronic gear seldom escape damage even when the lightning protection system works perfectly.

SPECIAL NOTE

Grounding of metallic objects for lightning protection may increase the possibility of harmful galvanic corrosion. Additional cathodic protection of the vessel with sacrificial zincs or other methods may be required.

Personal Safety

Even when the boat is properly protected, the crew must observe special precautions during lightning storms:

1. When possible, remain inside a closed cabin or under permanent shelter.
2. Avoid making contact with any hardware or metal pieces attached to the lightning protection system. If contact is necessary, avoid allowing the operator to bridge the gap between two such objects. (For example, do not touch a lifeline stanchion when cranking a sailboat winch.)
3. Do not allow swimming during lightning storms. Arms and legs must *not* be dangled in the water.
4. Sailors should avoid contact with metal spars, shrouds, stays, fittings, and railings.

ADDING A 115-VOLT OUTLET

Time: One to three hours.

Materials: Duplex outlet, nonmetallic junction box, plastic or wood cover plate, 12-gauge boat-cable wire, crimp connectors, solder. For surface wiring: plastic raceway and surface mounting box, mounting screws.

Tools: Saber saw, electric drill motor, drill bits, screwdriver, pliers, wrench, wire cutters, crimping tool, soldering iron.

Safety: Never work on live 115-volt AC circuits. Always disconnect power before doing any work on existing circuits.

There is a tendency among boat builders to install only the minimum number of 115-volt AC outlets. Adding an extra outlet is not difficult work, though to route the wiring correctly can be time-consuming. But it's time well spent, because the safety of the crew depends upon the work being done correctly.

The easiest way to add an outlet is to extend the circuit to an existing outlet. Turn off power to the existing outlet before beginning work. (To be absolutely sure the boat's 115-volt system is "cold," unplug the shore cord and secure the on-board generating set.) Remove the existing outlet from its box and let it hang on the wires that feed it. Thread the new cable into the bottom of the existing junction box from the bottom, leaving 6 to 8 inches hanging out the front of the box next to the receptacle. Always use at least 12-gauge stranded wire (boat cable).

Snake the cable through the interior furniture or behind headliners to reach the location of the new outlet. Snaking cable takes patience and a bit of ingenuity. Keep in mind that the cable should be supported every 18 inches with an approved cable clamp. Be sure not to route the wiring through the bilge or any compartments that may contain fuel tanks.

Mark the location of the new outlet and drill ¼-inch holes in the corners of the cutout. Connect the holes with a saber saw to get a neat, round-cornered cutout. Mount the nonmetallic junction box behind the cutout and run the wire in through the bottom.

Sometimes the only way to reach a location is by surface wiring. Special plastic wire chases and surface mounting junction boxes are available from home-improvement stores for this purpose. They come in a white that matches household baseboards and a brown that matches no known wood. The raceway consists of two pieces, a backing strip and a snap-on cover. The backing strip is mounted to the bulkhead and the wires inserted behind the cover. A variety of inside and outside corner pieces allow the raceway to go

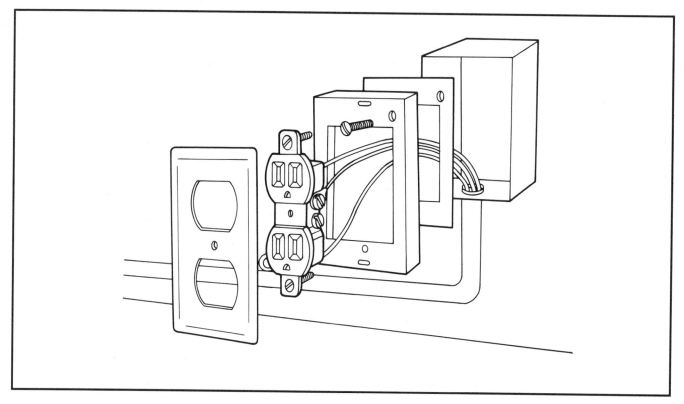

Shore power outlets (120-volt AC) add convenience to dockside living. Only twisted wire boat cable should be used. Solid copper house wiring is not acceptable. The wiring should enter the bottom of the box, and crimp-on eye connectors should be used to attach the duplex outlet.

around bends. Surface-mounted outlet boxes have special cutouts to accept the raceway. Ordinary duplex receptacles and cover plates fit these boxes.

Always use captive spade lugs on the ends of the three wires (black, white, and green) in 12-gauge boat cable. These lugs connect to the screw terminals on the outlets. Lugs must be crimped to provide a solid mechanical connection. They can also be soldered in an attempt to prevent corrosion. Never pinch the strands of the wire directly under the screw of the terminal. Always use an approved crimp connector lug for mechanical strength.

Duplex receptacles have extra screw terminals for adding an extra outlet down the line. Use these terminals to connect wires from the existing outlet to the new one. Be sure to follow the standard color code: white wire to nickel (silver) terminal; black (or red) wire to brass (gold) terminal, and green wire to the green ground lug.

Once the wiring is done, carefully push the receptacles back into their respective boxes. Screw them down, then install cover plates. Ordinary plastic plates will work, but teak or mahogany cover plates add a real touch of class.

Safety Considerations

Keep in mind that while adding an outlet adds convenience, it does not increase the capacity of the circuit. The total amperage on the circuit still must not exceed the rating of the fuse or circuit breaker. Outlets on the exterior of the boat or in the galley or head compartment should be of the GFCI (ground fault circuit interrupter) type to protect against accidental electrocution. Exterior outlets also must be in weatherproof boxes.

Always hook up all three wires: the hot (black or red), the neutral (white), and the ground (green) for safety. For full details on proper wiring of 115-volt AC circuits, see ABYC standard E-8.

12-VOLT OUTLETS ADD CONVENIENCE

Time: One hour.

Materials: 12-volt outlet, wire, in-line fuse holder, crimp connectors.

Tools: Electric drill motor, spade bore or hole saw, screwdriver, wire stripper, crimping tool, pliers.

Safety: Observe caution when drilling through panel where wiring is hidden.

The automobile cigarette lighter has established the standard for 12-volt outlets and plugs for cars, recreational vehicles, and boats. Spotlights, inflator pumps, and a variety of other 12-volt appliances come equipped with plugs intended to fit an automotive cigarette lighter outlet. Marine-grade outlets are available to make 12-volt power available almost anywhere it is desired. Not surprisingly, these outlets come with a cigarette lighter that often has a built-in chart light.

Before drilling any holes, measure the depth of the outlet to be sure there is enough clearance behind the panel. Twelve-volt outlets extend well behind the panel in which they are mounted. Also, be sure that it is physically possible to route wires to the location selected. As always, measure twice, drill once.

The outside diameter of the outlet is usually between 1⅛ and 1¼ inches. A spade bore of the correct size does a good job of cutting the mounting hole in wood panels. Use a hole saw for cutting through fiberglass. Dry fit the outlet to be sure that it fits. A file or rasp may be necessary to clean burrs or rough spots in the hole to allow the outlet to seat properly.

Twelve-volt outlets use a variety of connections

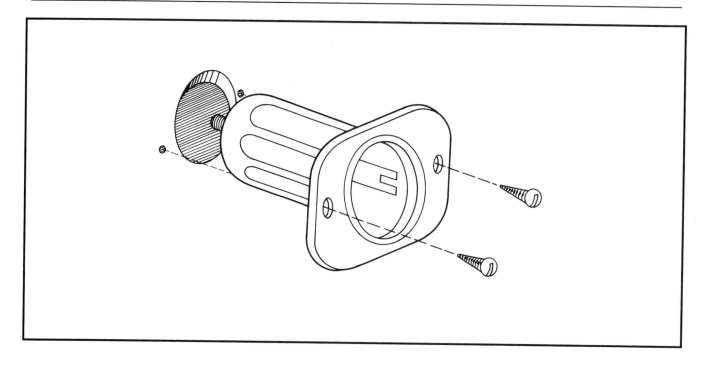

The 12-volt outlets used on U.S. boats are based on automobile cigarette lighters. Installation is simply a matter of drilling the correct size hole and pushing the outlet into place. The red (+) positive lead should go to the center post of the outlet, while the black (−) negative lead attaches to the outer shell. An in-line fuse should be used in the red wire.

that vary with the manufacturer. Captive spade lugs should be used on wires attaching to screw terminals. Insulated female plugs are used on studs. Crimp connectors tightly to the feed wires to prevent high-resistance connections. Don't scrimp on the wire gauge. Spotlights, hair-dryers, and cigarette lighters gobble up electricity. Sixteen-gauge is the minimum to use with a 15-amp fuse, and 18-gauge wire should not carry more than 10 amps.

Polarity is critical when installing a 12-volt outlet. Many of today's electronic devices (TV sets, CD players, computers, and so on) can be seriously damaged if the polarity of the DC power is reversed. The positive (+) red lead must *always* go to the center terminal on the back of the outlet. The negative (−) or ground lead must *always* connect to the outer shell of the outlet. If in doubt about the correctness of the polarity, check it with a voltmeter.

Outlets must always be fused in the positive (+) lead. They may be connected to any existing circuit, although serious consideration should be given to overloading. For instance, the boat's interior lighting circuit may become overloaded by a large spotlight. Overloading can be avoided by wiring the outlet directly to the output of the boat's main battery selector switch. In this case, an in-line fuse is required in the positive (+) wire.

⚓ AUTOMATIC BILGE PUMPS

Time: Sixty minutes.

Materials: Float switch, pump control switch, wire, heat-shrink tubing, mounting hardware.

Tools: Electric drill motor, drill bits, wire cutters, wire stripper, pliers, wrench, soldering iron.

Safety: Beware of explosion hazard when using spark producing tools in the bilge of gasoline-powered vessels.

Float switches are used to actuate automatic electric bilge pumps. Wiring one to an ordinary electric bilge pump allows the pump to automatically remove water from the bilge. The switch may be installed either next to the pump it controls or at some remote location. Float switches are often forgotten by boat builders, especially on smaller craft, where price is a major consideration. Adding a float switch is not a major project, even though there are some special safety considerations.

The switch is normally located in the lowest part of the bilge adjacent to the pump. Use the bracket and mounting hardware supplied with the switch to mount it on a stringer or bulkhead. The float switch must be wired in series with the positive (+) 12-volt wire (normally color-coded red). If there is any uncertainty as to which wire is positive, test with a small voltmeter.

An automatic bilge pump is the only piece of electrical equipment normally not disconnected when the main battery switch is turned off. It is wired directly to the boat's battery so that it will continue to dewater the bilge even when the boat is not occupied. Wiring around the battery switch, however, presents the possibility that the pump

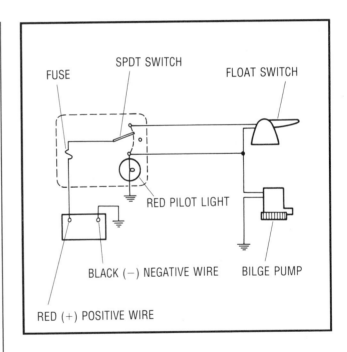

Proper wiring of an electric bilge pump allows total control from the helm station. A single-pole, double-throw switch can either turn the pump on or energize the float switch for automatic operation. A "center off" position on the switch cuts all power to the pump when that is desired. The red pilot light is optional.

will drain down the battery by continuous operation. If this happens because the *bilge is always refilling with water*, the boat should be hauled for repairs.

A less likely reason for the pump to run continuously is the failure of the float switch to shut off when the bilge is dry. Running dry can cause serious damage. If a damaged pump rotor stalls the motor, a serious fire hazard develops. The only way to protect the boat is with a fuse of the proper size in the positive (+) wire to the pump. Always use a fuse of the rating specified by the pump manufacturer.

CORROSION ALERT

The pump will appear to be operating correctly if the switch is installed in the negative (−) wire. However, in this arrangement power is constantly applied to the pump motor. The pump will not run when the switch is open, but power on the motor raises the possibility of serious corrosion. Stray currents from the pump could cause electrolysis of engine components in contact with bilge water.

Pump Control Panel

Special control panels are available for automatic bilge pumps. These usually combine a fuse holder with a three-position rocker switch and a pilot light. In the "manual" position, the control panel switch feeds power continuously to the pump, bypassing the float switch. In the center "off" position, the panel switch shuts off all power to the pump. In the "auto" position, the panel feeds power to the float switch for automatic operation. The pilot light comes on whenever the pump is operating.

Three wires are required from the control panel to the pump. One is the negative (−) wire from the boat's electrical system. This should be unbroken from the pump connection to the boat's negative bus bar. The standard color for this wire is black. The other two wires are the positive (+) power feeds. One power feed goes from the "manual" terminal on the panel directly to the pump. The other goes from the "auto" terminal to the float switch and then to the pump. Both of these wires should be color-coded red. Always use the gauge of wire specified by the pump manufacturer.

The main positive (+) feed to the control panel is normally connected to one of the battery connections on the back side of the main battery switch. A crimp-on ring connector should be installed on this wire. If the boat has two batteries, connect the pump to only one of them. The other battery should be protected from being discharged by continuous operation of the pump.

Waterproof Connections

Wires and connections between wires are normally not allowed in the bilge where they might get wet. This is obviously impossible with an electrical bilge pump, which must be located where water will collect. Special care should be exercised when installing a pump or float switch simply because the wiring may be submerged from time to time. Connections must be waterproof.

Heat-shrink tubing (available, for example, at Radio Shack) can be used to seal soldered joints. Cut a length of this tubing and slide it over one of the wires before the joint is soldered. Then, when the joint has cooled, slide the tubing down over the joint and use heat from the soldering iron to shrink it tightly.

Ordinary electrical tape is not satisfactory for protecting joints in the bilge. Over time the sticky stuff on this tape loses its grip and water enters the connection.

INDEX